Simon Jenkins is a write edits *Ship of Fools*, the the community, which has lau as the Mystery Worshipper a 3D church complete with .... avatars and celebrity preachers, Church of Fools. Simon's previous books include *When Clergymen Ruled the Earth* (Kingsway, 1991), *The Bible from Scratch* (Lion, 2015) and *Windows into Heaven* (Lion, 1998), an introduction to Eastern Orthodox icons. He writes a monthly humour column for *Reform*, the magazine of the United Reformed Church. Simon tweets as @simonjenks and lives in London.

Jumble Sales of the Apocalypse

Written and illustrated by
Simon Jenkins

Mark + Lois,
1,000 blessings (approx.)
Lots of love,

SPCK

First published in Great Britain in 2017

Society for Promoting Christian Knowledge
36 Causton Street
London SW1P 4ST
www.spck.org.uk

The publisher and author acknowledge with thanks permission to reproduce extracts
from the following:
'Raptor' by R. S. Thomas is reproduced by permission of Bloodaxe Books.
Every effort has been made to seek permission to use copyright material reproduced in this
book. The publisher apologises for those cases where permission might not have been sought
and, if notified, will formally seek permission at the earliest opportunity.

Two Scripture quotations are from the Authorized Version of the Bible (The King James
Bible), the rights in which are vested in the Crown, and are reproduced by permission of the
Crown's Patentee, Cambridge University Press.
One quotation is from the Holy Bible, New International Version (Anglicized edition).
Copyright © 1979, 1984, 2011 by Biblica (formerly International Bible Society). Used by
permission of Hodder & Stoughton Publishers, an Hachette UK company. All rights reserved.
'NIV' is a registered trademark of Biblica (formerly International Bible Society).
UK trademark number 1448790.

Permission is given for the cartoons to be reproduced free of charge in church magazines and
other not-for-profit church literature, provided that the following acknowledgement is used:
Jumble Sales of the Apocalypse (London: SPCK). Copyright © Simon Jenkins 2017.

British Library Cataloguing-in-Publication Data
A catalogue record for this book is available from the British Library

ISBN 978–0–281–07721–2
eBook ISBN 978–0–281–07722–9

Typeset by Simon Jenkins
Manufacture managed by Jellyfish
First printed in Great Britain by CPI
Subsequently digitally reprinted in Great Britain

eBook by Fakenham Prepress Solutions,
Fakenham, Norfolk NR21 8NN

Produced on paper from sustainable forests

Jesus came proclaiming the kingdom,
and what arrived was the church.

(Alfred Loisy)

Contents

Thanks

The forty pieces in this book started life as a monthly column in *Reform*, the magazine of the United Reform Church. The editor, Steve Tomkins, invited me in 2013 to write comedy pieces for their back page, so a percentage of blame must go to him for their existence. As well as being grateful to Steve for the opportunity to write, I'm also in debt to Charissa King at *Reform*, who has always been big on both encouragement and timekeeping. Those two qualities don't always go together, and I'm thankful for them both.

I don't want to hog this page like a tired and emotional celeb at an Oscars microphone, but I must also say thanks to the Facebook people who read my pieces when I posted them each month. I've appreciated the praise, and with time I've also appreciated the (usually well deserved) bollockings. And finally, a thank you to the very nice people who run the Café at Foyles in Charing Cross Road, London, and the Chelsea Café in Bath, where many of these pieces (plus the cartoons) were first sketched out.

1
Lives of the
coin-operated saints

Even though I've been a Christian for several centuries (well, so it sometimes seems), I must confess I've never seen a saint smacking himself in the face with a crucifix before. It happened when I went to London's National Gallery to see a wonderfully eccentric art exhibition called *Saints Alive*. The artist behind the show, Michael Landy, is very taken by all the pictures of saints in the National Gallery's vast collection of paintings. Inspired by them, he's made huge statues of his favourite saints which alarmingly clank into life when visitors press the right buttons. Each saint is noisily mechanical, powered by a Heath Robinson collection of pram wheels and old motors rescued from skips.

St Francis is my favourite in the show. He looks just like your average Catholic statue, gazing lovingly at a crucifix he holds close to his eyes. But pop a coin in the slot, and the crucifix abruptly smacks him in the face. Just nearby is a torso of St Jerome connected to a muscular arm holding a big rock. It's an alarming-looking thing, towering 12 feet tall. You stomp on the fat red button on the floor, and the arm bashes the rock into the chest three times. Crash! Crash! Crash! The cartoon-like violence is taken directly from the letters of St Jerome, where he confided that he found this the most effective way to take his mind off the dancing girls of Rome.

All this might be completely Monty Python, except that Michael Landy seriously admires the saints. Maybe it's because of his Catholic upbringing, but he's attracted by the way these unusual characters pursued the extremes of self-sacrifice to the point of death. He likes the way they went against the culture of their times: 'The saints are all very single-minded individuals. That's what I like about them.'

The seven saints in the room, which also include Lucy, Catherine and Thomas, are so vigorous in their self-inflicted punishments, I'm worried they're going to smash themselves to bits. And in fact, the St Lucy Lucky Dip, which has a mechanical grab which you can use to win a free t-shirt bearing the slogan, 'Poverty, Chastity, Obedience', is out of action. I ask one of the National

Gallery attendants about it and he says there's always one saint on a break, because he or she is broken down and waiting for a new part. 'It's all very well making them out of old junk from car boot sales,' he says, disloyally, 'but when they're being activated hundreds of times a day, they just wear out.' That's a bit annoying for visitors, but it's the point of the show: the contraptions break themselves down, just like the saints.

Celebrating the value of faith by highlighting the comedy of its wilder excesses strikes a chord with me. That's because I've been on a similar (but obviously much lowlier) track ever since I invented a magazine called *Ship of Fools* back in the late 1970s. The *Ship* went on to become a website and discussion board community at the turn of the millennium, and still sails the high seas of the Net. It's where Christians can be refreshingly self-critical about their religion, which they love but also question. And less seriously, it's also a place for collecting holy shopping items such as the Talking Tombstone, 'What Would Jesus Do' boxer shorts and fluffy loo covers printed with the words, 'Let my people go'.

I hope these pieces have some of the same comedy-critical eye. They started life as a monthly column in *Reform* magazine, with the sensible name, 'Jumble Sales of the Apocalypse'. The humble jumble sale and the almighty Apocalypse of St John don't obviously have much in common, except they are both part of the Christian faith. A huge amount of attention has rightly been paid to the Apocalypse and all the big things of Christianity, such as Bibles and bishops, creeds and conflicts, synods

3

and saints. But there's also genuine value in looking at the small and neglected things, including jumble sales, pious loo covers and the everyday realities of the spiritual life. They might be brilliant or embarrassing, classy or kitsch, but they tell us important stories about who we are, how we live as believers now, and whether we make sense to the wider world.

The things I'm writing about are a bit offbeat, like St Jerome with his rock. As Malcolm Muggeridge once said, 'Humour is the disparity between human aspiration and human performance.' That's why the Church is often one of the funniest places on earth, because our aspirations are so high. And it's what I'm going to explore, in the pages that follow this one.

2
Pulp testimony

One of the first books I read after I became a teenage Jesus freak in 1970 was a paperback by Nicky Cruz, a 1960s gang leader from New York who became a Pentecostal preacher. Unlike the more worthy books put in my hands at the time, *Run Baby Run* was a racy read, with lashings of sex, drugs and rock'n'roll, backed up by guns and flick-knives, and it kept me turning pages late into the night. It was a pulp-fictionalized version of reality, with dialogue that couldn't possibly have actually happened, because the protagonists would have been too stoned, drunk or angry to have remembered it.

The thing that turned this salacious stuff into righteous reading was the steady drip-feed of fearless preaching and tearful conversions to the Lord amid all the glamorized violence and excitingly sinful goings-on. And thus it came about that my introduction to Christianity was also an introduction to a sort of soft porn. It was like opening a bottle of fizzy Communion wine that had just been handed you by an arm-waving charismatic.

Come to think of it, I encountered an author of pulp testimony the night I was converted, at a crusade evangelism meeting in Cardiff. The evening was a heady mix of sacred solos, melodramatic preaching and a testimony from Doreen Irvine, whose salvation from a life of Satanism and paid-for sex was detailed in her ghost-written autobiography, *From Witchcraft to Christ*. Doreen's story should never have been allowed anywhere near the non-fiction shelf, as it was as shaky as a pulpit balanced on a couple of cocktail sticks. She hobbled to the microphone to say that, backstage, the Devil had pushed her down some stairs to stop her testifying. But, she said, the Old Nick was going to have to do a lot better than a sprained ankle to stop Doreen.

The godfather of pulp testimony was David Wilkerson, a Pentecostal pastor who wrote *The Cross and the Switchblade*, the most famous book in the field, also about taking the gospel to New York gangs. It's shifted 15 million copies since it was published in 1962 and has been made into a movie starring Pat Boone. That's a little reminder that in its heyday, pulp testimony generated serious money for authors and publishers and launched lucrative speaking careers. The success of Nicky Cruz and David

6

Wilkerson created a powerful temptation for others to come up with their own bankable testimonies.

One person who embraced that temptation with a great big bear hug was Crying Wind, who wrote about growing up in poverty on a Kickapoo Native American reservation before she found Christ. Her eponymous book became a bestseller, and she toured churches in full Indian costume, which was a thrill for her believing audiences. The trouble was, Crying Wind was actually a white, well-educated woman called Linda who didn't even look like a Native American, but did have a talent for passing fiction off as fact. The publisher, who should have read the smoke signals a lot earlier, investigated and pulled the book. One Christian leader joked they should have renamed it *Shooting Bull* and kept selling it as fiction. I was working for the publisher of the UK edition at the time, and our favourite rechristening of it was *Lying Wind*.

But in a plot twist which shows that fictionalized testimony is stranger than . . . er . . . fiction, another publisher with bargain-basement ethical standards picked up the book, and by 1980, Crying Wind was back in business. She continued touring in native costume and inspiring Christians with her fake stories.

In 2004, a new contender hit the market. It had kung-fu, car chases, organized crime, Chinese punishment beatings and prison violence – all the things Christians apparently want to read about, shame on us. The book was *Taming the Tiger* and the convert was a man calling himself Tony Anthony. His career in violent crime ended in a Cyprus prison, where he says God finally caught up with him.

That would have been a wonderful turnaround for Mr Anthony (although not much consolation to the people he damaged along the way) if the colourful details of his former life were at least on nodding terms with the truth.

Tony Anthony shifted 1.5 million copies of his book and built a career of speaking in schools, churches and prisons around the world. But his story had so many holes, plagiarisms and contradictions that the Evangelical Alliance, called in as an honest broker, concluded that Anthony's 'true story' wasn't. And that's where the *Crying Wind* plot twist kicked in again. After Authentic Media (actual name) pulped the book, another publisher snapped it up, ironed out the most obvious bloopers, and Tony Anthony was back from the dead, like a Christian zombie.

You'd think Christian publishers would learn. But maybe some of them have learnt, and drawn a profitable conclusion.

Dear God, I **wish** to **complain** about your non-**existence** in **the** strongest **possible** terms

God, Nowhere

3

The new new atheists

Twitter has its fair share of parody accounts, where scamps posing as Justin Welby, Pippa Middleton or Elizabeth Windsor share their deeply inappropriate thoughts. One of the consistently most fabulous is a tweeter with the nom de guerre of KimKierkegaardashian. His or her tweets are a satire on the empty celeb lifestyle of Kim Kardashian, the reality TV star whose career has predictably oozed over into clothing and perfume collections. The tweets mangle the star's vacant thoughts with the downbeat philosophical observations of gloomy Dane Søren Kierkegaard. This produces gems such as: 'I love facial treatments. While one's immortal soul is disintegrating, they make you feel rejuvenated and refreshed.'

It used to be that vanity, celebrity and materialism were attacked with lip-smacking relish from pulpits up and down the land every Sunday morning, and hardly anywhere else. But these days, philosophy is also taking on the job. In fact, philosophy is making a very credible bid for the religious franchise. This has been happening since 2008 at The School of Life, which offers classes, books and Sunday sermons designed to help people dodge the vices and embrace the virtues of life today.

For £15 a pop, you can sit under the ministry of preachers as eminent as Ruby Wax, Terry Eagleton and Grayson Perry, who have respectively taken as their subjects the ego, evil and kinky sex. (I hope churches in search of an eye-catching new sermon series are taking notes here.) The service in which the sermon is delivered is full of ironic, churchy details such as tea ladies in aprons and wigs, pop songs sung as hymns, and a pantomime Devil in a tight red suit and floppy horns who invites you to confess your sins. Five hundred people belting out 'Eye of the tiger' is apparently a welcome change to dirgeing along to 'The day Thou gavest'.

The headmaster of The School of Life is the philosopher Alain de Botton, who is quite a different kind of atheist from the new atheists. Richard Dawkins, new atheist in chief, might give brilliant lessons in the biology lab, but when he's deputizing for double RE on a Friday afternoon, he gets things muddled up and shouts a lot. By contrast, Dr de Botton is all charm and soothing reasonableness. His book, *Religion for Atheists*, even gets flirtatious with religion, flattering the dear old thing by saying she's given us wonderful stuff such as community, morality, art, education and consolation in the face of death. The trouble is, religion has also given us God. So de Botton suggests we plunder religion for its priceless human value while chucking away its worthless supernatural content.

After the Dawkins years, in which we believers were told our faith was a mental illness, this nuanced approach to religion seems at first glance like a good thing. It's refreshing to hear de Botton being so nice about religion, even if it's the kind of compliment a thief offers before stealing your wallet.

So what happens if you follow de Botton's advice and take the religion out of a Sunday service? For churches located in the stratosphere, with thuribles spinning, bells tinkling, deacons bowing, jewelled crosses being marched from A to B and priests scuttling behind screens, there wouldn't be much left without the religion, aside from the after-service gin. But for a low church service, with the minister in jeans and jumper, the sermon replaced by standup, and a spot or two of worsh-u-tainment from the band, religion could quietly slip out of a side door without anyone really noticing it had buggered off.

I got the chance to test out a religionless service when I went to the opening of atheist church, the Sunday Assembly. We stood to sing our first hymn. I was hoping it would be that rousing Victorian standard, 'At the name of Hitchens, every knee shall bow', but instead we had Sam Cooke's 'Don't know much about history'. Following that was a sermon, some quiet reflection, more singing, large amounts of very good comedy, lashings of strong tea, and a congregation of 250 who had to queue up before they could get in the door. It also included no God at all, but also nothing about religious people being deluded. Instead, we celebrated 'the sheer wonder of being alive'.

Which is the greater threat to faith: the mockery of Dawkins or the gentle persuasion of de Botton and the new new atheists of the Sunday Assembly? The question is hard to answer, because what persuasion has produced is attractively human. It's created communities of people who want to talk and reflect on life and its meaning. They just don't want God to be part of it. And that's the start of a much more interesting conversation than we ever had with the old new atheists.

He's always
believed in Dog

Elbib
†

4
Love me, love my dogma

Do animals go to heaven? Will there be mewing, woofing and squeaking on the streets of the New Jerusalem? Are dogs not just for Christmas, and not just for life, but for eternity too? Theologians have only occasionally bothered their planet-sized brains about this weighty question, which these days is raised whenever a blogger loses a much-loved cat, dog or budgie. I should know, since I blogged about my dog Sasha when she went for walks with the angels.

For the enrichment of this piece, I tried to find out whether any of the great theologians actually kept a pet, hoping against hope to discover that the prim John Calvin kept a raucous, red-bottomed baboon. But the Google search kept getting distracted by words such as 'dogma', 'catechism' and even 'rabbi'. I was pleased, though, to discover that the German theologian and medical missionary Albert Schweitzer was very attached to Parsifal, his pet pelican, whom he adopted when the pelican's mother was shot, and that he observed: 'There are two means of refuge from the miseries of life: music and cats.' And talking of cats, it was good to be reminded of St Jerome, who allegedly removed a thorn from the paw of a lion when it limped into his monastery one evening. The lion was so grateful that it shared Jerome's study while he translated the Bible into Latin.

Meanwhile, talking-animal enthusiast C. S. Lewis had three pets at the end of his life: Ricky the boxer, Snip the cat, and a ginger tom (called Tom) whom he described as 'a great Don Juan and a mighty hunter before the Lord'. Lewis's positive approach led him famously to speculate that animals which relate to humans would have a share in eternal life. His attitude is a bit of a contrast with that of Bernard of Clairvaux, who popularized the saying, 'Love me, love my dog' – *Qui me amat, amat et canem meum* – several centuries before it became a top ten hit. The saying might sound like a warm invitation to cuddle up to my pooch, but in fact is intended to mean that if you love me, you have to accept everything about me, even the ghastly bits – which is hardly a compliment to my dog.

It took another St Bernard (St Bernard of Montjoux) to atone for that insult by giving his name to the breed of brandy-bearing dogs used by monastic communities high up in the Alps to rescue pilgrims stuck in the snows on their way to Rome.

The reason I started thinking about all this is because I spotted a new book, *Truly Devoted*, by devotional writer H. Norman Wright. The book cover, decorated with bones, kennels and pawprints, features two grinning, panting retrievers and has the subtitle: *What dogs teach us about life, love and loyalty*. It is, verily, the perfect Christmas gift for the dog-obsessed Christian, with chapters drawing life lessons from how dogs gnaw bones ('Our worries are the same. We bite and chew on them'), obedience training ('How do you respond to God's request to be obedient?') and even a dog's big nose ('Look in the mirror. How do you feel about yourself?'). This is all well and good, except for the danger of sentimentalizing animals, which props up our abuse of everything below us in the food chain. Turning the lives of animals into parables casts them as sweet and adorable creatures who exist merely to serve their human masters.

That kitschy approach is very much on display in a new trend: pet baptism and confirmation services. Earlier this year, one New Yorker took her miniature pinscher for confirmation in a church service involving godparents and a confirmation gown. This followed in the footsteps of a Pet Baptizing Kit sold on eBay, which came complete with holy water, a baptismal certificate, a prayer (of St Francis, naturally) and instructions for a ceremony that will 'enrich the lives of both you and your pet'. My feeling is that if this trend really takes off, it will soon split in two, with some dogs going for a sprinkle at the font (so to speak), while others choose full immersion in a baptistery, followed by a jolly good shake and a roll on the church carpet.

I'm sure kittens have earned their place in paradise if only for the work they do in pointing people to the Lord via the medium of the cheesy poster. One example I saw recently shows a tiny tabby peeking out from behind a sunflower, while the text burbles: 'Be patient. God isn't finished with me yet.' Not one to view on a full stomach. Perhaps we're asking the wrong question. Rather than, 'Will animals go to heaven?' we should be asking, 'How on earth can they live with us?'

We mow it
every spring

5
Jesus shaves

Beards have been bristling into the news headlines in the past few months. Jeremy Paxman's decision to give his razor a rest last summer proved as much of a gift to journalists as David Dimbleby's session in an East London tattoo parlour. The viewing population of *Newsnight* quickly polarized into pro- and anti-beard and Paxman passed it all off as 'a storm in a shaving mug'.

Then baby-faced Gareth Malone turned up for the filming of the BBC's *The Choir* with an unexpected ginger specimen of the topiarist's art clinging to his face for dear life, which triggered fresh storms of outrage and adoration on Twitter. Both of them became contenders in Beard of the Year, an annual wag-off between the mightiest beards of the kingdom. At the time of writing, John Hurt, the only bearded Dr Who ever, is leading the list with almost 39 per cent of the vote.

I only raise the subject because a package arrived from Amazon and it got me thinking about the connection between hairiness and holiness, as well as the tragic decline of the beard in church life. The package contained a satirical little item called the Jesus Shaves Mug. I took it in the kitchen to test it out. It is adorned with a Jesus who would look perfectly at home in a Sunday School, complete with long hair and flowing beard, except for the fact that he is brandishing a pair of scissors. I popped in a tea bag and added boiling water and within seconds the familiar facial hair of our Lord miraculously faded away to reveal a clean-shaven Saviour, bearing an eerie resemblance to an Italian hairdresser.

There was a time when beards covered a multitude of chins. There was Moses and St Paul. There was Nebuchadnezzar with his knitted beard and Pharaoh with a little wooden goatee held in place with the Egyptian equivalent of elastic. There was Elijah and Jeremiah and other monumentally angry Old Testament saints. There was Leonardo and Michelangelo. There was Santa (and come to think of it, his anagram, Satan). In the nineteenth century, a golden age for facial fungus, there was Marx and Darwin, both much bushy of face. C. H. Spurgeon, the celebrated Baptist preacher, who was given to smoking a soothing cigar after sermons, even said: 'Growing a beard is a habit most natural, scriptural, manly and beneficial.' His own beard was a living testament to that doctrine.

The Victorian century was a time when the beard could stride forth into the world with a biblical swagger, knowing it would be greeted with reverence and respect. In fact, the Victorian beard was so almighty that your face under that heap of hair might have been less visible than a woman in a niqab. But that high tide of beardiness has now withdrawn. The day of the omnipresent beard is now sadly passed. The big, biblical beard is no longer king. It's true that the hipster beard has tried to turn the clock back, but it's the exception rather than the rule. All that remains are the bearded chops of Rowan Williams.

In its heyday, the beard was theological. When did you last see a pope with a beard? Or an Orthodox archbishop without one? For the record, the most recent bewhiskered pope was Innocent XII, who sported a jaunty goatee plus moustache until the end of his reign in 1700. He ended 150 years of popes who wore beards in defiance of a church law which decreed that priests should keep their faces shaved. Apart from that lapse, the Romans always preferred to follow the example of Jacob in the book of Genesis: 'Behold, Esau my brother is an hairy man, but I am a smooth man.' Around the turn of the first millennium, papal bulls and excommunications were issued against clergy who dared to follow the way of Esau.

The insistence that all Roman clergy should be clean-shaven gave the Protestant Reformers a splendid opportunity of showing how rebellious they were. Many of them, bad boys such as John Knox, Menno Simons and Thomas Cranmer, all previously Catholic priests, grew beards as their theology shifted. And all the while, the Eastern Orthodox clergy maintained their impressive face rugs, believing that smooth faces meant you were just a big girl.

All of which seems irredeemably trivial, not to mention irrelevant to the female half of the human race, just like quite a lot of church history. Until you remember that God officially has a big white beard (it says so on the ceiling of the Sistine Chapel) and Jesus always has a hairy face himself, even if it's a bit bum-fluffy. This popular image of a bearded deity somehow conditions how we imagine God to be. Maybe the beard is more ticklish than we think.

I think it must
mean peace in
our time

6
This never happened to
John the Baptist

The vicar was in a bit of a flap, because of a radio mic malfunction. It was the start of Morning Prayer at a church in Cornwall, and everyone was ready to launch into the first hymn, but the poor cleric at the front was rummaging around in his vestments, trying to locate the microphone lead. It wasn't a good look. Spotting the problem, the sound desk guy sprinted up the aisle, knelt down behind the vicar and adjusted the lead. 'Er, it's all right,' said the hapless priest to the congregation. 'He's just turning me on.'

Human miscalculation in the religious life can sometimes leave a church congregation rocking with laughter, but of course it isn't always like that. Take just two mishaps in the past few weeks which found their way into the media. In the first, the doves of the Vatican came under attack – and for once that's not a reference to liberal modernizers in the Roman curia. Two children released real, cooing doves from the Pope's window overlooking St Peter's Square, to huge applause from the crowd below. But then a crow and a seagull swooped in and suddenly the doves of peace were being pecked by the seagull of doubt and the crow of derision. In other words, the intended symbolism of the moment got rather lost.

The press coverage was bad enough, but then animal welfare groups started lecturing the Pope on the folly of releasing domesticated birds into the avian rough-house that is Rome, and Pope Francis was probably left reflecting on how this never happened to John the Baptist. This pope does have amazingly good luck, though, because just a day later a man in the St Peter's Square crowd offered the Holy Father his pet parrot, who hopped onto the Pope's finger and said 'Papa!' What are the chances that a pilgrim would bring his parrot to see the Pope? Those Vatican spin-doctors have everything covered, don't they?

But the second religious mishap I noticed in the media was a lot more theological and fascinating. Someone had the bright idea of scripting a text message conversation between Jesus and an iPhone user and putting the screen-shot into an evangelistic leaflet. The edifying conversation went back and forth like this:

Hey
What's up
We need to talk
Can it wait? I'm kinda busy
That's the problem. You seem too busy for me
I'll make it up to you. Maybe tomorrow

But a problem arose when a sharp-eyed user of the social media channel Reddit noticed something not quite right. The texts were meant to be started by Jesus, trying to get a distracted believer's attention, but the bubbles were the wrong way round. Suddenly it looked like the believer was trying to get heaven's attention, but Jesus was, like, 'whatever'. This triggered a flood of comedy and comment on Reddit. Some users were intrigued by why Jesus was so distracted. 'Jesus, are you seeing someone else?' asked Human_Sandwich, while MisterWoodhouse suggested Jesus' next text: 'Trying to beat my Father's high score in Candy Crush. The guy is godlike at this game . . .'

But alongside all the banter, small discussions of issues arising started to crop up. There was a flurry of debate about prayer. An argument about the Trinity started with mockery but became quite educational. Some users cast doubt on whether Jesus ever actually lived, and others pointed to the historical evidence. And there was some to and fro about free will, which ended up with one user quoting the philosopher Alvin Plantinga. It got to the point where a user called teeelo asked: 'Wouldn't it be great if the creator of this ad knew exactly what they were doing?'

Sometimes things go wrong in our communication and it leads to laughter or criticism, rather than the things we were hoping for. But maybe more often than we think, positive things spin out of it as well, such as genuine conversation and encounter, as happened here. Our crazy mistakes can reveal our flawed humanity and draw people to us, or else create an opportunity for the Pope to meet a parrot. Comedy, especially the gloriously unintended kind, isn't a distraction from salvation, but an essential part of it.

My vicar once told me about a bishop, dressed in all his finery, about to give the blessing at the end of a cathedral service. The deacon assisting popped on the bishop's big pointy hat, but accidentally got it backwards, so the lappets (the long ribbony bits) hung over his face. As the wretched deacon desperately tried to rotate the hat, the bishop calmly placed a hand on his arm and said, 'No, don't. Let them see what fools we are!' That's the spirit.

Would you care for some After-Hate Mints?

7
The seven deadly chocolates

Mars and Flake, Twix and Galaxy, KitKat, Milky Way and Aero. They are the seven deadly chocolates in churches up and down the land each spring. Have you ever thought how much Cadbury's must hate Lent? It's no wonder Easter positively wallows in chocolate eggs after all that self-denial.

The middle weeks of Lent are always a bit of a low point. Whether you gave up Facebook, Marmite, Jeremy Kyle or one of the above chocolate temptations for the six-week run-up to Easter, the chances are that by now you sincerely want them back in your life. Especially if giving them up way back on Ash Wednesday was a heat of the moment thing, spiritually speaking. Asking people how they're doing with Lent several weeks in feels the same as asking them at the end of January, 'How are those new year's resolutions coming along?'

Of course, as we're always told, Lent isn't just about giving things up. It's also about taking things up: getting out of bed extra early to pray, being nice to your ghastly boss, reading the book of Leviticus, forgoing the joy of cutting up other drivers at the lights. But actually, giving things up is still where Lent cuts the deepest. It's only when we seriously try saying no to 'brother body', as St Francis endearingly called it, that Lent becomes the blessed bloodbath it's meant to be.

Lent could be easier if people were more familiar with the small print. I've often found that not everyone knows you can have Sundays off, for example. The reason being that every Sunday is a celebration of the resurrection – and is therefore an opportunity to praise the Lord by getting alone with a party-sized pouch of Maltesers. Some churches, such as the Ethiopian Orthodox, also take Saturdays off to make a weekend of it, but then they have to compensate by having a colossal eight-week Lent to get in the full 40 days of fasting.

This year, noted believer Ann Widdecombe announced her Lenten cutbacks (which surely takes points off her Purgatory loyalty card for the sin of boasting). 'As usual,' she thundered, 'it will be everything except fizzy water to drink: no alcohol, tea, coffee, cola or fruit juice.' Her list of privations made me realize that the items people drop for Lent are quite individual and sometimes eccentric. Fizzy water might be exempt from Ann Widdecombe's list, but why is that? It's not as if Jesus went into the wilderness with a bottle of San Pellegrino.

I checked on how our Christian forebears tackled things back in Victorian times and was thrilled to discover they invented the Lent book, with its mixture of pop theology and sober advice on what to give up and what to take up. Their preoccupations are a world away from KitKat and fizzy water. 'Can it be fitting that any of the Lord's disciples should be marrying or giving in marriage whilst He is lonely and fasting in the wilderness?' asked Charles Kennaway (rather melodramatically, to my mind) in his twopenny booklet of 1849, *How Lent May be Kept by Rich and Poor*.

The Revd William Kip agreed and noted that the same principle extended to celebrating birthdays, which were 'inappropriate to a season which should be devoted to deep humiliation and mourning'. Thank goodness Revd Kip's own birthday was in October, and therefore unaffected by his dictum. Meanwhile, Bishop Jeremy Taylor, writing about almsgiving, advised that 'many things might be spared; some superfluous servants, some idle meetings, some unnecessary and imprudent feasts, some garments too costly, some unnecessary law-suits, some vain journeys'. I was so glad to read the bishop's words. Lent just wouldn't be Lent unless you sacked a few of the servants.

A Catholic bulletin board reveals the things people fasted from in 2014: selfies, French fries, playing basketball, saying OMG, coffee 'which is the fuel of my life', McDonald's, sex, rock'n'roll, 'animal based products including honey', lottery scratch cards, Justin Bieber, anger, 'listening to music (excluding Gospel)', pizza, online shopping, lying, cursing and poker websites. It's a highly specific list which shows how the temper of Lent has changed since Victorian times, and also reveals the mundane habits and inner demons which assail modern Westerners.

Lent is just 40 days out of the year for most of us, but for others it has been and is a chosen way of life, with eccentric saints living on top of poles, monks and nuns who take on 'poverty, chastity and obedience', and believers who forsake home and comfort to live and work in the world's most needy places. The condition of many people living on earth today can be described as Lent without Easter. It's for them that we should have more Lent in our lives, the whole year round.

8
Name that church

I came across a story a while ago about an evangelical organization looking for a snappy new name for their ministry to students. They were impressed by the kung-fu style name of CICCU (the Cambridge Inter-Collegiate Christian Union), and at a meeting they brainstormed ideas for names along those lines. But the session ground to a halt when someone helpfully suggested, 'How about the Fellowship of Universities and Colleges Christian Unions?'

The story is probably apocryphal, although stranger things have happened in the Christian world. Such as the Nairobi church I discovered the other day called Helicopter of Christ. I couldn't help quipping about it on Twitter, and someone immediately tweeted back with: 'Mock all you like, they will just rise above it.'

Church names have got a bit out of hand in recent years. It used to be so simple: you had a saint who once lived locally or you admired (or you thought would help stave off the next bit of Viking pillaging) and you named your church after him or her. You slapped in a few wall paintings of St Cuthbert or St Dorothy and that was it. Job done. A book published 100 years ago contains a league table of medieval English church names. Apparently St Mary leads the field with no less than 2,335 churches to her name. St Peter comes in second with less than half that number at 1,140, while St John the Baptist and St Mary Magdalene lag behind with a mere 500 and 187 churches apiece.

Admittedly, some churches tried to get creative within this predictable system. A London church rejoicing in the name of St Ursula and the 11,000 Virgins, for example, once occupied the site where the Gherkin now proudly rears heavenwards. And if that isn't a sign of the times, I don't know what is.

However, the churches I knew when I was growing up in the 60s and 70s had no saints' names. That's because I was in South Wales, and the churches were Congregationalist, Baptist or Calvinistic Methodist. I got to know them quite well because (tragically for them) I started preaching at 18 and was sent by my Baptist church in Cardiff up the valleys on Sunday mornings to visit these great and gloomy temples of the Lord. Each church had only a sprinkling of old people sitting in the yawning acres of pews, plus a deacon or two dressed in Bible black. They were the final survivors of the 1904 Welsh Revival, and as they listened to the dire preaching of 18-year-old me, it must have been final confirmation that the glory had not just departed, but had danced off on holiday to Benidorm in a sombrero, never to return. Once I'd finished my sermon and descended from the Mt Sinai of wood which was the pulpit, a deacon's hand would stray into my jacket pocket to deposit a crumpled envelope containing a fiver.

The names of these churches always impressed me: forbidding names such as Tabernacle and Ebenezer; mountain names such as Moriah, Hermon and Carmel; names of places where prophets and patriarchs had met God, such as Ararat, Bethel and Zion. The Welsh revivalists who named these chapels were very taken with Old Testament encounters with God and wanted their grand and grumpy buildings to deliver the same experience. Since those times, church names have risen and fallen with the tides of spiritual fashion. The dress-down, hippy 60s gave us names which pay homage to the bearded, sandal-wearing believers of those days: Vineyard, Mustard Seed, Ichthus, Potter's House. They were names beloved by the bran, brown bread and breastfeeding brigade.

That's also when some of the churches named after saints went hip and trendy by resorting to nicknames. The Church of Saints Philip and Jacob, Bristol, became 'Pip n Jay', while St Andrew the Great, Cambridge, morphed into 'Stag'. If anyone knows of a church dedicated to Saints Thomas and Jerome, but calling itself 'Tom and Jerry', please let me know.

Today's hipster churches of the Western world have determined that pompous is the best way to go when you're getting your name and logo together. Where once you might have gone to St Paul's Church or Salem Chapel, you'll now find yourself in The Edge, Ikon, The Pursuit or Empower. Meanwhile, churches in Nigeria are pushing in the opposite direction with brilliantly tasteless names such as Guided Missiles Church, Healing Tsunami Ministry and (possibly the best church name of all time and eternity) the Happy Go Lucky Church of Almighty God in Jesus Name Amen.

However you choose to name your church, one trend above all others is definitely worth keeping an eye on. The New Jerusalem Church in Little Bolton changed its name several years ago. It's now called Bolton Carpet Warehouse.

9
The dove was a ghost

In the history of the movies, a medium not noted for its devotion to things religious, it's surprising how often nuns grab the spotlight. Who could forget Maria von Trapp, the singing sister, trilling among the edelweiss in *The Sound of Music*? Or the rather more burly figure of Sister Mary Stigmata expertly whacking her young charges with a ruler in *The Blues Brothers*? And then there's Sister Mary Clarence, a lounge singer hiding in a convent, who teaches the choir to sing gospel in the movie *Sister Act*. But out-

nunning all other nuns on the silver screen are Sisters
Euphemia and Inviolata, played by Robbie Coltrane and
Eric Idle, in the British comedy *Nuns on the Run*.

Euphemia and Inviolata are actually two bank robbers
disguised as nuns, who hide out in a convent to escape a
spot of bother in gangland. They quickly realize they have
to know something more than how to hold a crucifix the
right way up if their disguise is going to work. And that's
how they end up trying to get to grips with the doctrine
of the Holy Trinity. The crook posing as Sister Inviolata
(Robbie Coltrane) had a Catholic upbringing, so he starts
them off.

'You've got the Father, the Son and the Holy Ghost. But
the three are one – like a shamrock, my old priest used
to say. "Three leaves, but one leaf." Now, the Father sent
down the Son, who was love, and then when he went away,
he sent down the Holy Spirit, who came down in the form
of a . . .'

Euphemia (Eric Idle) interrupts: 'You told me already –
a ghost.'

'No, a dove.'

'The dove was a ghost?'

'No, the ghost was a dove.'

'Let me try and summarize this: God is his son. And
his son is God. But his son moonlights as a holy ghost, a
holy spirit, and a dove. And they all send each other, even
though they're all one and the same thing.'

'You've got it. You really could be a nun!'

It wouldn't be much of a stretch to say that you might
overhear exactly this conversation in a church near you

this month. And that's because the middle Sunday of June is Trinity Sunday. The very name stirs up fear in the bowels of even the most seasoned preacher. One church minister told me the other day that everyone she knows avoids almost to the point of death preaching on Trinity Sunday, because whatever the preacher says will leave the congregation more bug-eyed than ever about the subject. Ministers have been known to arrange their holidays across the dreaded Sunday, or failing that to produce an implausible sick note, or cite a distant relative's funeral, or claim that zombies are surrounding their house – anything, in other words, to make the sermon fall on someone else's head. And that's because the punishments for failing to take one of those courses of action can be severe.

An Essex minister who bravely waded into the doctrine in his sermon last year was immediately held up for all to see on Twitter. A member of his congregation tweeted: 'Possibly the phrase "living in a threesome" may not be best way to explain the Trinity.'

When I was a child, congregations were still required to stand up and recite the tangled and tiresome Athanasian Creed, which requires you to say: 'The Father incomprehensible, the Son incomprehensible: and the Holy Ghost incomprehensible. And yet they are not three incomprehensibles, but one incomprehensible.' Which only goes to show how church can be even funnier than films about bank robbers posing as nuns. It wasn't always like this, though. In the time when the doctrine of the Trinity was put together, way back in the fourth century, it aroused huge amounts of passion and debate.

The doctrine's chief opponent, the Egyptian presbyter Arius, turned his arguments against the Trinity into pop songs. His catchy, 'There was a time when the Son was not' was so infuriatingly hummable that the fathers of the Council of Nicea stuck their fingers in their ears rather than listen to its seductive words and sexy tune. Arius ended up being smacked in the face by St Nicholas (yes, that's dear, loveable Santa Claus) and being labelled the worst heretic of all time.

So if the Trinity today arouses parody in movies, bewilderment in pews and truancy in pulpits, it's worth remembering that it once had the power to enthral, divide and finally bring together the young Church. And since 'In the name of the Father . . .' is spoken in most churches each week, it's something that's worth trying to understand. We could do worse than follow the splendid example of Sisters Euphemia and Inviolata in struggling with it, even if we end up with 'The dove was a ghost?'

Let's sing verse 10,002 again!

10
Not very English

I got into a bit of a tangle with worship this past week. A friend who works on Stephen Fry's *QI* for BBC Two invited me to join the studio audience for a recording, and in the green room afterwards, while I was grazing on Doritos, I was introduced without warning to one of the gods of comedy.

Imagine a deity who shaped *Not the Nine O'Clock News*, *Spitting Image*, *The Hitchhiker's Guide to the Galaxy* and *Blackadder*, and you're thinking of John Lloyd. He produced them all. Shaking his hand, I meant to offer a brief, 'Hello, thanks for tonight's show,' but to my horror found my mouth burbling a profuse hymn of praise for all he'd done o'er the years and how much better my life was because of his wondrous works. In my mental replay of the grim scene, the crowded green room falls silent, except for the sound of someone gagging in the corner.

I should have followed American humourist Garrison Keillor's advice on how lowly consumers like me should approach the great and famous. No speeches, no pursuit, no physical contact, no trying to get the awesome one to read your bloated, unpublished manuscript. Just a brief and casual, 'Love your work. Means a lot to me,' and leave it at that. Worship should be understated because it's just embarrassing all round if someone recites your praises at length with flowery grandiloquence.

Anyway, back home, I started thinking about it. I realized there's an exception to the general rule that worship should be downplayed, because there's someone who never tires or gets embarrassed about hearing his praises sung at length, ideally with choirs warbling and organs thundering. And that is the Lord. Indeed, if the chorus of non-stop worship falters even fractionally, then the psalms kick in by insisting that every creature and every musical instrument must get back to the job of praising his name. Psalm 150 even breaks into exclamation marks over it, which is a rarity in the Bible.

I'm not for a nanosecond disputing that God deserves the best kind of glory and adoration there is. It just seems curious that he loves it so much and that he gets highly vexed and jealous if worship goes to false gods such as

Baal, Zeus or Justin Bieber. I bet that if God has a TV programme he always sets to record, it's *Songs of Praise*. It all seems highly uncool and not at all modest or English of him.

I first noticed this when I watched the movie *Monty Python and the Holy Grail* back in 1975. In a scene I couldn't help warming to despite the fact that I was a keen teen believer, the clouds part and God, in a top-heavy crown, addresses King Arthur, who has fallen to his knees. 'Don't grovel,' says God testily. 'If there's one thing I can't stand it's people grovelling.'

My mind boggles when I hear preachers say there will be just one item on the programme in heaven: worship for literally countless ages. I'm sure Charles Wesley was getting something important right when he put 'lost in wonder, love and praise' into one of his hymns, but hymns are pretty much history now. Instead, an eternity of worship conjures up teenage guitars, songs on endless repeat, and lyrics which talk about Jesus as if he was a slightly insecure boyfriend who needs constant declarations of saccharine-flavoured love. Then I'm not so much lost as mislaid in worship. People often say they have a problem with hell, but I have a problem with heaven. How can a loving God sentence people to an eternity of singing, 'Oh, oh, oh, how good is the Lord'?

I realize all this might be making a rather big hole in the middle of my faith. It's a God-shaped hole, and not in a good way.

Maybe worship is like people who visit Niagara Falls and stand with their mouths hanging open as they watch that colossal curtain of water drop to the rocks below. They're reduced to animal-like grunts of wonder. These days, of course, the default response to any shocking (or even mildly surprising) moment is a shrieked 'Oh my God!' – which kind of makes my point for me. Just key 'Niagara Falls OMG' into YouTube and you'll see what I mean.

Or maybe worship is like a person about to jump in front of the 7.15 to Basingstoke, but saved from doing it by a timely rugby tackle from a fellow traveller. Years later, in her right mind, she can't help saying thank you over and over to her saviour. Awe and gratitude, I'm sure, are the psychological heart of worship. But I still think it's not very English when God seems to enjoy it so much.

Pass as you would
have it be passed
unto you

11
Ask Jesus

Twitter waxed theological one Monday afternoon a few weeks ago, thanks to that noted school of biblical studies, Manchester City Football Club. The club was doing some social media PR and invited fans to tweet questions to their Spanish right-winger, Jesús Navas. They sensibly chose the eyecatching hashtag #AskJesus for the task, and that whipped up the kind of Christological frenzy that hasn't been seen since the Council of Chalcedon.

The flood of tweets which followed included enquiries such as: Is it more fun playing for Man City or healing lepers? Can you explain why you walk on water but dive on grass? What are you like on crosses? Who do you hate more: Judas or United? If you can turn water into wine, can you turn Javi García into a decent footballer? Was that really you in my tomato?

There was something here for everyone: blasphemies to make the descendants of Mary Whitehouse reach for the 'smite' button; puns more painful than watching England lose on penalties; and little jokes for preachers to copy and paste into the intro for this week's sermon. The hashtag quickly accelerated to 93 tweets per minute, making #AskJesus the No. 1 trending topic in the UK.

The calculated mixup between Jesús Navas and Jesus of Nazareth isn't anything new. Like all famous Jesi, Navas has been the plaything of newspaper headline writers since the start of his career. Just a year ago, his winning penalty for Spain in a game against Italy was greeted with: 'Praise Jesus!' Meanwhile, his namesake Jesus Luz, a Brazilian fashion model who dated pop star Madonna, was doubly blessed by a headline which announced: 'Madonna trying for a baby with Jesus'.

Google turns up many famous people called Jesus: footballers, wrestlers, a folk musician, several politicians, a (now deceased) drug baron and more baseball players than you could shake a bat at. All of them are from countries speaking Spanish or Portuguese. In fact, the name is so plentiful in South and Central America that a post on a forum I visited recently asked the genuinely perplexed question: 'If Jesus was Jewish, how come he has a Mexican name?'

Jesus has apparently been chosen as a first name in the Iberian countries since at least the fourteenth or fifteenth centuries, and according to one theory, it's because Spanish and Portuguese piety is so in love with the holy family. José, Maria and Jesus are all popular choices at the font, with José and Maria topping the lists for Spanish boys and girls for much of the twentieth century. Another theory holds that because Spain and Portugal were part of an Islamic state until only a few hundred years ago, Christians living there might have called their boys Jesus in imitation of Muslims who called theirs Muhammad.

The name Jesus has never been on the baby name menu in the English-speaking world. Unusually, the French agree with the English on this point. A French synod in 1692 said that priests should stop people calling their children names 'ascribed unto God in Scripture, such as Immanuel, and others of like nature'. Today, there's no legal prohibition in Britain from calling your baby Jesus, but it's more likely to happen in a register office than at a christening near you. Curiously, English-speaking Christians avoid the name for exactly the same reason that Spanish-speaking Christians embrace it: reverence for Jesus himself.

Last summer, a couple living in Tennessee got into hot water when they gave their baby boy the name Messiah. A judge ordered the name to be changed, saying that Messiah had been earned by one person and 'that one person is Jesus Christ'. She added that the name Messiah could cause problems if the child grew up in Cocke County, which has a sizeable Christian population. To my mind, Cocke County has enough problems of its own, namewise, to start laying down the law about baby names, but maybe that's just me.

Another place where baby naming got out of hand was the Mexican state of Sonora, where the registrar issued a list of 61 prohibited names, based on what parents had actually been calling their newborns. They included Lady Di, Robocop, Facebook, Christmas Day and Circumcision.

Given the brilliance of Latin footballers, wordplays linking our Lord with the beautiful game are unlikely to cease – and in any case they have something of a history. In 1964, a church near Liverpool city centre posted a pious question on its Wayside Pulpit: 'What shall we do when the Lord comes to Liverpool?' A day or two later, a fan of Bill Shankly's team responded with a scrawled message: 'Move Ian St John to inside left.' It'll take a £15m transfer fee at least to make that happen now. Either that, or the Second Coming.

12
Gideon's camouflage Bible

I didn't know before just now that Gideon Bibles – the ones you find in hotel rooms – are colour-coded, just like tube lines and Daleks. There are red Bibles for school pupils. Orange for the victims of street evangelism. Green for uni students. White for medics. Camouflage for soldiers. And Bibles covered in little black arrows for convicts. OK, that last one isn't strictly true. Or even at all.

The camouflage edition for troops is a new development in the legendary relationship between Bibles and bullets. I thought this only went back to the First World War, but it actually dates from Oliver Cromwell's New Model Army.

In the stories, an incoming bullet finds a Bible in a soldier's jacket pocket and rips all the way through to the book of Ecclesiastes before it is stopped, hallelujah.

The filmmaker Woody Allen has a similar testimony. Years ago, he says, his mother gave him a bullet, which he kept in his breast pocket. 'One day, I was walking down the street, when a berserk evangelist heaved a Gideon Bible out a hotel room window, hitting me in the chest. That Bible would have gone through my heart if it wasn't for the bullet.'

The Gideons have been dishing out free Bibles since 1908, starting as a mission to help travelling salesmen behave themselves in hotels. They're expecting to give away their two-billionth in the next year or two. In recent times, the Gideon Bible has faced tough competition. Back in the good old days, the Bible in the drawer was the only form of entertainment in the average hotel room, but now it has to compete with the mini-bar, wifi, flatscreen TV and the porn channels.

Surely the days are numbered when businessmen gratefully turned to the book of Obadiah for some improving reading before crashing for the night. And yet half of all the Bibles the Gideons have ever produced in the century since they started have been given away in the last 15 years. So they must be doing something right. The fact they got name-checked in a Beatles song, 'Rocky Raccoon', has to count for a lot too, although the Gideons themselves would probably disagree. They're a highly conservative organization, and won't even allow women to join them as full members.

The reason I noticed the many colours of Gideon is because their Bibles have been taking a hit in the news lately. They were basically dropped by Travelodge in the summer, who cleared all the Bibles from their rooms and popped them into a forgettable cupboard behind reception. The hotel chain, in an unusually theological moment, said they didn't want to 'discriminate against any religion', even though no religion had put in a complaint. If anyone wants a Bible, they said, they can ask Wayne on reception to fish one out of the cupboard if he can find the keys. This prompted Premier Inn to smugly issue its own creed: 'Bibles are available in Premier Inn rooms.'

The last time the Scriptures were forced to vacate their rooms, they were replaced with copies of ghastliest book of all time, *Fifty Shades of Grey*. The manager of the hotel in Cumbria which made the switch explained, 'The Gideon Bible is full of references to sex and violence,' and the rest of his sentence is so banal and unfunny that I won't bore you or me with it.

Meanwhile, national treasure and incarnation of Gandalf, Sir Ian McKellen, admits to a habit of ripping pages out of hotel Bibles whenever he opens a bedside drawer. Says Sir Ian: 'It's Leviticus 18.22 that I object to: "Thou shalt not lie with a man as with a woman. It is an abomination." I think the punishment for being abominable was being stoned to death. I don't think those are very comfortable words to have at the bedside of someone passing a lonely night away from loved ones.' Ironically, Gideons and Gandalf are united in wanting to bring spiritual comfort to lonely travellers, but disagree over whether the Good Book actually does it.

Comfort offered itself in a rather unexpected way to one businessman, who checked into his room one evening with a heavy heart as he was feeling lonely and missing his wife back home. He found the Gideon Bible beside his bed, opened it and read: 'If you're sick, read Psalm 38. If you're in danger, read Psalm 91. If you're lonely, read Psalm 23—' That's me, he thought, and turned to the lovely words of Psalm 23. As he finished reading, he found a scrawled note at the bottom: 'If you're still lonely, call Fifi on 202-126-0311.'

The Gideons should take Fifi and Sir Ian McKellen as a compliment. Indifference, not editing, is surely their biggest enemy.

13
A bone to pick with relics

I went to Rome a few years ago, just after Papa Benny got the top job. Despairing of the gargantuan queue for the Sistine Chapel, I descended instead into the bowels of St Peter's, where they have a lot of old popes in storage – each of them, I'm sure, hoping someday to ascend, at least into the basilica. I paid my respects at the rather neglected tomb of dear Pope John Paul I, the 'smiling pope' who sadly died in 1978 after just 33 days in office. But in the middle of doing that I got distracted by a hullabaloo at the tomb next door, where a scrum of pilgrims was jostling around the slab of new star arrival, Pope John Paul II.

The heavies of Vatican Security were there in force, determined to keep the flock moving, but they faced Polish women brought up under 40 years of Communism. Delving into their handbags, the women produced handkerchiefs, not to mop away tears, but to press against the walls of the tomb. I suddenly twigged that new relics were being minted before my eyes. They were low-grade items, as they hadn't been in contact with JPII himself, but what went back into the handbags were Holy Hankies.

The thing about Holy Hankies is they can command a price. It's always been thus: relics and money go hand in hand. I checked the truth of this very easily a few days ago by window shopping on eBay. What I found would have set Martin Luther rotating in his grave like a cement mixer. For just $98, I could have a piece of clothing worn by St Jude the Apostle. For $350, I could buy a piece of the True Cross. 'This Cross has been divided in many parts now,' oozes the blurb with no apparent irony. It reminded me of John Calvin's celebrated satire on the relic trade, which observed that Europe had so many pieces of the True Cross, they could rebuild the ark. Best of all, for $1,200, I could buy a glass locket containing pieces of the cradle of Bethlehem and the tomb of Christ. Praise the Lord and pass the credit card!

Geoffrey Chaucer, who wrote *The Canterbury Tales* 600 years ago, would have instantly recognized these eBay knockoffs. 'You would have me kissing your old breeches, And swear they were the relics of a saint,' he mocked.

Risible relics might seem like a medieval hangover, but the fraudulent old trade is doing very nicely, thank you.

One surprising development is the relic rock tour, with ancient body parts being lugged around the globe for the faithful, exactly like a Rolling Stones tour. Back in the day, the pilgrims travelled to the relics, but now the relics come to you, and millions get the chance to venerate them. The thigh and foot bones of St Thérèse of Lisieux, a nineteenth-century French nun, have had an extraordinary career since the turn of the millennium, playing to packed churches in Australia, Ireland, the Philippines, Russia, Iraq, the United States, England and Wales. They even dropped in on South Africa for the 2010 World Cup. And now the saint's writing desk has launched its own career, with a US tour last year. First stop: Las Vegas.

The big tours this year included a tubeful of St John Paul II's blood, on a road trip between Boston and Florida; a bit of the ankle of St Toribio, a Mexican priest of the 1920s, touring California; and a statue of Our Lady of Fatima, which has embarked on a gruelling three-year tour. It can only be a matter of time before the skis of John Paul II are spotted on the pistes of the French Alps. Meanwhile, the shinbone of St Mary Magdalene, on a much-needed break this year, has been given a new reliquary. It's exactly the right size for hand luggage on Ryanair. Also resting are the sandals of Blessed Mother Teresa.

I don't have a Protestant's objection to relics. The last time I visited St Mark's in Venice, I sought out the high altar, under which the bones of St Mark himself, the writer of my favourite Gospel, are said to rest. Standing near the sarcophagus, on which are the confident words *Corpus divi Marci evangelistae*, I unexpectedly found myself thanking Mark for bearing witness to Jesus, and then realized that technically I was praying to a saint. It felt as natural as texting a friend.

So if I have a bone to pick with relics, it's a funny bone. Because while fake relics are being flogged on eBay and real relics are jetting off on celebrity tours, they remain comically out of joint with the wider world of Western culture. Whether that's so much the worse for relics, or for Western culture, is another question.

14
Badvent calendars

Standing in the queue for the checkout at Tesco a few weeks ago, I was eyeing up the impulse purchase items stacked around the tills and wondering whether to go for a 'two for the price of one' pouch of Maltesers, when my eyes fell on something that looked strangely familiar. Bang in the middle of the National Lottery scratchcard display, between the Lucky Dog and Win Pig cards, was a £5 offering called 'Christmas Advent Calendar'.

Forgetting the Maltesers for a moment, I leaned in for a closer look. It was an Advent scratchcard. There was Santa, standing in the middle of a snow-covered village, complete with a little church and sleepy houses. Each house could be scratched away to reveal instant cash prizes of up to £250,000. I must confess, my mouth fell open. The last time I paid this much attention to an Advent calendar was when I was a kid, and the only thing the calendars of those days coughed up was a piece of cheap chocolate that instantly stuck to the roof of your mouth.

At the risk of confusing the feasts of the Church, it was an Epiphany moment for me. Surely, I thought, the Three Kings didn't trudge all the way 'from Orient are' to Bethlehem over sand dunes so that Camelot could flog £25 million worth of scratchcards? This little revelation at the Tesco tills was one of the things that prompted a few of us on the satirical website Ship of Fools (which I edit) to launch a search for the year's worst Badvent calendar – the calendar furthest away from the original Christmas story. Our readers enthusiastically nominated the ghastliest specimens they'd seen, we selected a shortlist of the top eight, and then put them all to an online vote.

The list included a Lego Star Wars Advent Calendar, complete with Darth Vader dressed as Santa. It's the nativity story according to the Gospel of Luke Skywalker. I actually liked another entry – the Advent Calendar for Dogs – which has doggie-safe chocolate treats so your pooch can prepare for Christmas too. And then there was the Whisky Advent Calendar, with a different dram of hooch every day, at a price which suggests the manufacturer has confused Herod with Harrods: £150.

Advent calendars have a surprisingly short history, and they've always been a commercial product, so no one can really complain that they've been wrecked by greedy supermarkets in their ceaseless quest to squeeze every last drop of goodness out of Christmas. It was only in the nineteenth century that people in rural Germany started counting the days of Advent by adding a chalk mark on a door each day, putting up little religious pictures or burning a candle.

The first printed calendar, produced in Munich in 1908, was the opposite of a scratchcard. Not only could you not win a fortune, but you stuck pictures on, rather than scratching them off. Its inventor, Gerhard Lang, said that when he was a boy, his mum stuck 24 candies on a piece of cardboard for a calendar. He was from rural southern Germany, where religion tends to be sweet, kitschy and traditional. It looks like Advent calendars were always a mixture of sweets, surprises and stories, with the earliest calendars picturing elves, toy soldiers and fir trees among the Christmas angels.

You could say that today's calendars have stayed true to what Gerhard Lang was doing. They've just swopped the sweets for brands such as Star Wars and Dr Who, and they tell stories that children really want to hear. But it's depressing that no Advent calendar on the UK market tries to tell the first Christmas story, or gives anything to charity, or uses Fairtrade chocolate. They all seem to operate entirely outside the spirit of Christmas. Except for one: The Real Advent Calendar, which is worth a Google.

Meanwhile, back at our Ship of Fools Badvent calendar poll, we finally announced the calendar most likely to make the Baby Jesus cry. Scooping over 50 per cent of the vote, and knocking the dependably vacuous Barbie Calendar into third place, was the Ann Summers Advent

Calendar. It features a young chap with no clothes on, relaxing against a Christmas tree, having gift wrapped the only thing he could think of . . . in fact, the only thing he could ever think of. If the Christmas tree he's leaning against is real, rather than fake, then he must be sitting on a carpet of pine needles, which might explain why his come-hither expression looks more like an anguished cry for help. And behind each window of the calendar? The gold, frankincense and myrrh of Christmas has been replaced by chocolate willies, boobs and bums.

I guess we should be grateful. Ann Summers has reminded us that reproductive organs were literally part and parcel of the original Christmas story.

15
Oh em gee

Something curious happened on the Disney Channel website just before Christmas. Lilly Anderson, a girl from a good Christian family in North Carolina, visited the website on her tenth birthday and came across a question from Disney asking what she was most thankful for in her life. She keyed in: 'God, my family, my church and my friends.' When she clicked 'Send', she waited to see her message posted on the site, but instead got a little message in red which said: 'Please be nice!' It didn't take long for

Lilly and her mum to discover that they had to take the word 'God' out of the message for Disney to be happy.

This kicked up a veritable blizzard of 'Disney bans God' headlines in the right-wing press and reminded me of something I discovered on my smartphone a month or two earlier. I tried keying in an occasionally useful Anglo-Saxon word which rhymes with 'cluck' and found that my predictive text, which is normally so smug in trying to complete words ahead of me, simply folded its arms in righteous disapproval when it saw where I was going. It even offered words such as 'fudge', 'funny' and 'duck' to guide me back onto the straight and narrow.

Disney eventually had to come out and explain why it had upset Lilly. It turned out that hardly anyone posted God's name on the website in a 'Please be nice', North Carolina kind of way. Instead, they were posting 'God!' or, 'For God's sake!' or especially, 'Oh my God!' The problem was so bad, said Disney, that 'in an abundance of caution our system is forced to catch and prevent any use of the word on our websites'. Therefore Disney, emphatically, does not do God. This is borne out by the Parents Television Council (a conservative American TV watchdog which probably has Mary Whitehouse as its patron saint) which has apparently counted the number of times 'God' is spoken on primetime US television and says that 95.9 per cent of it is not what you would want your Bible-loving grandma to hear.

Today's casual profanity of choice is 'Oh my God!' It's used like a comma in everyday speech and has carved out an online career of its own as 'OMG'. I first noticed just how much it was being used on *Changing Rooms*, the TV show from the early 2000s. Contestants unwisely gave their neighbours the opportunity to wreck a room in their homes with hideous wallpaper and knocked-together furniture that probably fell apart as soon as the cameras stopped rolling. The poor victims were blindfolded and led into their destroyed rooms for the 'reveal' by a grinning Carol Smillie, and 99 times out of 100, when the blindfold was whipped away, they shrieked out, 'Oh my God!!!' with three or more exclamation marks. Whether they were crying out to the Lord for help in their hour of distress, or were just mildly surprised, was always an interesting question.

Then when Brian Dowling was crowned the winner of *Ultimate Big Brother* in 2010, he repeatedly cried, 'Oh my God! Oh my God! Oh my God!' This not only tells you pretty much everything you need to know about *Big Brother*, but also shows how the phrase was brought to the small screen by reality TV shows.

OMG is right there in the psalms, of course. 'OMG, my soul is cast down within me,' says Psalm 46. 'Deliver me, OMG, out of the hand of the wicked,' urges Psalm 71. Except that in the psalms it's not OMG but 'O my God', a genuine cry for help from someone at the end of their rope. Today, it's been watered down to a handy phrase people reach for when they encounter something a little bit unexpected and need to ramp up their surprise for effect.

OMG has been picked up by everyone from physicists to Furby. Physicists, shocked to find a high-energy particle travelling close to the speed of light, jokingly named it the Oh-My-God particle, a name which has stuck. Meanwhile, parents thinking of buying a Furby for their kids have been troubled at news that the furry robotic toy occasionally squeaks 'Oh-em-gee!' It also develops a split personality, burps, farts and throws up, so oh-em-gee might be the least of the problems.

Saying 'Oh my God!' can be a problem for all sorts of people, from atheists worried they are betraying their atheism, to Christians anxiously debating whether the phrase is blasphemy and how they should respond when they hear it used all the time. And what about God himself? Maybe the constant shrieks of 'Oh my God!' from office parties and chat shows are like tinnitus in the divine ear, as God strains to hear genuine human cries for help.

I've been assigned the guardian angelship of Bear Grylls

Tough gig

16
Be an angel

It was a $4 milkshake, the Oreo Blaster. I've never had one myself, but apparently it's a shake that does serious damage, because at 930 calories the Oreo takes four solid hours to walk off. But on this occasion, it also inflicted serious wallet damage, because when the customer who bought it came to pay, he wrote in an extra $100 tip on the credit card slip. Next to that, he wrote '@tipsforjesus'.

A mysterious group of wealthy Americans has been leaving outrageously huge tips on ordinary meal bills for the past 18 months. Just after Christmas, one of them must have had the *Guinness Book of Records* scrambling to register the biggest tip ever – $11,000 at a bar in Phoenix, Arizona. 'Let's have fun with this one,' said the anonymous wonderworker, as he added the five-figure number to a bill that was for just $89. He then grabbed a snap of the bill and posted it on the group's Instagram account, @tipsforjesus, which has the tagline, 'Doing the Lord's work, one tip at a time'.

The online comments soon flowed in. 'Wow!' 'I can't even imagine!' 'Can I please get a tip? I am in need.' And, 'May The Lord bless you and everyone who's doing this a million times over. May your guardian angels keep you safe in your journey.'

Despite the Jesus language and the anonymity of the tippers, tipsforjesus isn't specifically a religious thing. But the pictures posted on the Instagram page show barmen and waitresses in something approaching religious ecstasy as they unbelievingly count those zeroes. They look like they've been entertaining angels unawares – and maybe they have. But where the angels of the Bible came bearing glad tidings of great joy, these new angels of consumerism come bearing American Express.

Angels of whatever brand are fundamentally mysterious. They arrive unexpectedly, saying things such as 'Fear not', or 'Behold!', or 'Now what's my PIN?' and disappear when their mission is accomplished. One author, Emma Heathcote-James, made an academic study of angel encounters at the turn of the millennium and wrote about them in her book, *Seeing Angels*. 'I heard from one man who was waiting to cross a busy road on his way to work,' she says. 'Seeing a gap in the traffic he stepped out, only for an elderly lady he'd never seen before to stretch her arm out in front of his chest with such force it prevented him from crossing. Seconds later a sports car sped past – which would otherwise certainly have hit him. He turned around to thank the woman, but she was nowhere to be seen.'

In another story, from rural Iowa, two elderly sisters were stranded on a quiet country back road when their car got a puncture. Within a minute or two, a car drew up behind them and out jumped a couple of young men with strikingly blond hair, blue eyes and white suits. (I know you're thinking this might turn into a Jedward story, but trust me on this.) The young men fixed the puncture, refused all offers of payment, and then sped away, their car getting brighter and brighter until it disappeared in a pulse of white light.

The disappearing angel legend got rather badly dented a couple of years ago when a priest dressed entirely in black turned up out of nowhere at a car crash in Missouri. He prayed with Katie Lentz, who was trapped in the car, and then abruptly left the scene without speaking to anyone else. The firemen attending were convinced he was an angel, especially as their equipment suddenly started working better the moment he arrived, with the result that Katie was freed. But then local priest Father Patrick Dowling went and spoiled it all. Instead of sitting at home in the presbytery with a beer and a bowl of peanuts, revelling in the nightly angel speculation on TV, he dropped into the hospital to visit Katie and put her straight about who prayed with her – which made her cry. 'I think it was the most disappointing moment of all that I wasn't an angel or something,' he said. No kidding.

Since angel stories, one way or another, appeal so much, maybe it's time to realize: you could be that angel. On the train, don't just idly watch as some dear granny tries to wrestle her bulging suitcase onto the luggage rack. Approach her with supernatural calm, say as little as possible, raise the case without effort, and as she takes her seat, glide smoothly into the carriage loo. She turns to thank you, and – lo! – you have returned to heaven. Random acts of kindness, performed with theatrical aplomb, could just be the new evangelism.

Alternatively, buy a milkshake and leave an archangel-sized tip.

Naked Bible
Reading FOR CHARITY!

I thought **he'd use**
a **pocket Bible**

17
Naked Bible reading

I was in synagogue the other day, marvelling at a reading
from the book of Genesis. It's not that I'm Jewish myself,
it's just that my dad has been the Gentile organist at a
Reform synagogue, Sabbath by Sabbath, for the past 60
years, and I like to go along with him, kippah clamped on
head, whenever I visit my home town. What caught my
attention this particular Saturday was the determination
that went into the reading from the Torah.

No less than three people were welcomed to the lectern,
with handshakes all round, while just the man in the

middle read the lesson in painstakingly careful Hebrew, the other two supporting him. He seemed to know that Torah scroll back to front, which is just as well, as you can't read Hebrew any other way. It made the average church reading look a bit thrown together and hope for the best.

The most memorable Bible reading of my life happened when I was still at high school in Wales. It was assembly, and we'd just recited the ringing Welsh-language version of the Lord's Prayer, when Ceri Price stepped up onto the stage for the Scripture reading. The hall went completely still, and not out of any reverence for the Word of the Lord. Ceri Price lived just round the corner from me but was a year older, and with her long brown legs, short skirts, peachlike complexion, smirking smile, smart putdowns and eyes which flashed blue fire, she could turn any boy's brain into porridge. Two hundred pairs of schoolboy eyes followed her anxiously onto that stage, where she started into Jesus' parable of the sheep and the goats.

She quickly reached the moment when Jesus addressed the sheep: 'I was thirsty, and ye gave me drink: I was a stranger, and ye took me in: Naked, and ye clothed me . . .' This produced some audible gasps for air from the back row. After all, even mildly suggestive words such as 'rude' or 'bare' caused sniggering in assembly. But Ceri wasn't finished. Now it was the turn of the sheep to ask Jesus: 'When saw we thee a stranger, and took thee in? or naked, and clothed thee?' Large numbers of boys around the hall now seemed to be having problems with their breathing.

Then Jesus turned to the goats to accuse them of not being there when he was hungry, thirsty, sick . . . and not forgetting naked. And then of course, the wretched goats had to have their say about it all and quiz our Lord on each of these particulars. By the time Ceri Price concluded that the wicked were going away into everlasting punishment and the righteous into the life of the blessed, all 200 boys were either weeping with laughter or in the throes of a hormonal breakdown. Ever since that emotional high point, church readings have for me been downhill all the way.

The incident raises the interesting question: what Bible readings are appropriate for reading out loud in church? That might seem a ridiculous sort of question, until you realize that different churches at different times have banished whole Bible books from the reading lectern.

Famously, Thomas Cranmer, Archbishop of Canterbury for Henry VIII, left out the book of Revelation, as well as the Song of Songs, when he first drew up his readings for the church year. In a way, you can see his point. The Apocalypse has visions of creatures with multiple heads (not to mention people swimming in lakes of fire) which if they had been written in the 1960s rather than biblical times would have been put down to too much LSD in the Kool-Aid. The Eastern Orthodox churches still exclude the book from reading in church.

Meanwhile, the Song of Songs was banished for being too hot. Even though Christians had been told for centuries that all that flirting and humping was actually between Christ and his Church, Cranmer must simply have looked at the opening verse in the English translation he had – 'That thy mouth wold geve me a kisse' – and thought: no way. Apparently, the Song of Songs was a very popular reading choice in the lonely monasteries of the Middle Ages, but that's monks for you.

I've often thought Bible readings in church are not appreciated enough as an entertainment and a sport. There are so many details to trip up the reader who forgets to do his homework the night before. Towns called Shittim. The command not to covet your neighbour's ass. Verses that sound like football scores: 'The king of Aphek, one; the king of Lasharon, one' (Joshua 12.18, if you're wondering). The story of the Ethiopian eunuch read by someone with a high-pitched falsetto. Taking a couple of people up with you to help out, just in case, sounds like a very sensible thing to do.

And 34thly, we just pray you would just really be with Jeff and that you would just . . . make this stop now

18
The 75 per cent rule

'This building is prayer conditioned,' reads the sign outside Ryde Methodist Church, on the Isle of Wight. 'God answers knee-mail,' says the sign recommending Vinings United Methodist in Atlanta, Georgia. What is it about prayer (and church signs) that makes Christians hang up their brains? I've always been fascinated by the odd things that happen when people pray out loud together – whether it's hogging the limelight in a prayer meeting, adopting a special voice to pray in a church service, or insisting on saying grace over a ghastly Big Mac and fries in motorway services, while people at the surrounding heathen tables look on in puzzlement.

The church I was married in, which happened to be of the Brethren variety, had a sweet, 80-something elder in a grey, three-piece suit who could always be relied on for rising out of his seat to give thanks for the wine at Communion. 'We thank Thee, Lord, for the luscious grape,' Mr Floyd would always say, pronouncing the word as 'looshus', in his gentle Warwickshire accent. It was a much looked-forward-to moment in the service.

Public prayer has its own peculiarities of language, of course, but they are as nothing when compared to our strange behaviour when we humans pray together. I was at a meeting of a Christian charity recently which opened with Ron leading us in prayer: 'Lord, help us to have focused minds and not to be distracted by anything else. Help us to really concentrate on' – and at this point, I realized I wasn't being led in prayer, but lectured. It happens at the end of lengthy sermons, too, where the preacher grabs an extra five minutes to continue riding his theological hobby horse almost to death. Prayer is often war by other means.

While some prayers are polemics, others turn delightfully into gossip. When William Gladstone went one Sabbath to a Presbyterian service in Scotland, the minister served up the following prayer: 'We pray Thee, Lord, of Thy goodness, to bless the Prime Minister of this great nation, who is now worshipping under this roof in the third pew from the pulpit.'

Ever been in a prayer meeting where others are praying so freely and piously, even getting in some major points of doctrine, that you decide to play it safe and keep your mouth shut? This strategy is fine for a while, until the terrible realization dawns that almost everyone has prayed. Even the introverts you can normally rely on to stay silent have given it a go. The iron rule of prayer meetings is that 75 per cent is the tipping point. After that, everyone has to pray, or their walk with the Lord has obviously gone off a cliff.

One of the besetting sins of public prayer is how middle class and polite we are with God. During the Spanish Civil War in the 1930s, an abbess got fed up when her prayers didn't work. She took a chisel to a statue of the Virgin Mary, chipped away until she broke the Baby Jesus off, and then told the Madonna she would give him back when her side had won. This is the kind of language the Mother of God understands.

An East End youth worker I know once told a teenager that whenever she was tempted by the Devil, she should rebuke him. The next week, she reported that she had directed Satan to 'piss off in the name of Jesus', and that it had worked a treat. I can't help feeling that blunt prayers, whether delivered by chisel or in Anglo-Saxon English, are highly effective in heaven, not to mention hell.

Someone recently sent me the story of a dear old saint (admittedly not the precise phrase used of her at the time) who habitually hijacked the church prayer meeting. Everyone's heart sank whenever Agnes opened her mouth to pray, because she made it her business to thank the Almighty – at length – for everything in her life. Until one day, when she started off as usual. 'I thank God', she said, 'for the beautiful weather we've been having, and I thank God for fellowship and friendship, and I give praise and thanks that we live in a land of plenty . . .' and so on and so forth.

After a solid ten minutes, she moved on to thanking God for her house and its contents. 'And I thank God', she said, 'for my dining room with its beautiful table, and I thank God for my wonderful fitted kitchen, but most of all I thank God for the little ray of sun that shines down my back passage.' At this point she faltered. And the vicar jumped in and said, very loudly and firmly, 'Amen.'

19
On holiday with the Lord

Where do you go to church when you're on holiday? Several years ago, my evangelical auntie, asking what I would be doing on my impending beach holiday, told me tartly: 'You may be going on holiday, but you can never have a holiday from the Lord.' Despite that precious truth, most believers, as far as I can see, don't go to church when they're abroad, especially if they're in a foreign-language country. There are good reasons for it, of course.

Going to an unfamiliar church requires nerves of titanium even when you speak the same language. This was the experience of George, who foolishly ventured into a Gospel Hall in Glasgow a few years ago. Quizzed at the door about his born-again credentials and the disappointing lack of a big black Bible under his arm, he was directed to an obscure corner at the back. Once consigned to the pews of the damned, he was excluded from the Lord's Supper, but looking on the bright side, he was also excluded from the collection bag. This rather chilly visit to church dropped to freezing point, said George, when 'the preacher stared in my direction in the far corner for the entire sermon'.

If that can happen in a church possibly around the corner from you, what horrors might await if you darkened the doors of a French Catholic, Greek Orthodox or Spanish Pentecostal church, all of them (especially the Pentecostals) speaking crazily in unknown tongues?

Despite the dangers, can I encourage readers to give church a go this summer holiday? I'm suggesting it because being in a service where you don't know the language is just an intensely interesting thing. You'd think it would be boring, but that's reckoning without fear. Fear keeps you alert, because at any moment you could find yourself standing when you should be sitting, or launching into a solo at the end of the hymn, when everyone else understood the instruction to omit verse five. That's when the entire congregation turns to inspect you, the person who has done the wrong thing, just like in the movies.

This actually happened to me when I went to an Ethiopian Orthodox liturgy. It was in London, but the service was spoken in Ge'ez and Amharic. I made myself walk into church confidently, as though I'd been there a thousand times before. I steered myself smoothly into a pew, sat down and bowed my head for a moment of pretend prayer. When I looked up, I discovered that I was the only man sitting in the women's section, with several women looking at me, and not in a good way.

The second fascinating thing about church in an unknown language is that you switch channel from the ear to the eye. The minister might as well be talking in Klingon, and so you begin to notice visual oddities that maybe the church regulars have never spotted. I visited the Thomaskirche in Leipzig a couple of years back, the church where J. S. Bach was once in charge of the music. As I sat in my pew, wondering why 'German' rhymes with 'sermon', I noticed something curious.

The pulpit was mounted on a pillar in the nave and was sideways on to the congregation. If the preacher stood squarely facing his notes, then he was facing the pillar across the nave from him. And on that pillar was a large old crucifix in tarnished gold which was mounted at a slightly lower height than the pulpit. This meant that the preacher was talking down to Jesus. Maybe the intention was to keep the cross of Christ ever before the preacher's eyes, but I think the Thomaskirche ought to sort it out.

And there are other joys to discover in your holiday churchgoing. Such as the handsome young priest, newly installed at a Catholic church in Bordeaux, who concluded a wedding I went to last summer with the exhortation: *Faire l'amour!* ('Make love!'). This blessed instruction was received so enthusiastically by the French congregation, with cheering and applause, that there was a real danger of it being put into immediate effect.

Meanwhile, in Croatia, at a charismatic service featuring flag waving, a forest of raised arms and outbursts of tongues, the congregation spontaneously started to sing, over and over again, 'Sweaty bog! Sweaty bog! Sweaty bog!' My friends, who witnessed this unlikely moment, were practically weeping with laughter, but their tears were fortunately mistaken for joy, since *Sveti Bog!* in Croatian means 'Holy God!'

Why miss out on these untold riches? This year, go on holiday with the Lord.

20
Ginormous Jesus

One night in 1977, American televangelist Oral Roberts had a dream about Jesus. The Lord commanded him to build a world-class hospital in Tulsa, Oklahoma, and as a sweetener promised to let Roberts in on the cure for cancer. So far, so normal, in the Magic Roundabout world of Pentecostal televangelism. But what sent the dream a little bit off piste was that the Christ he met was 900 feet tall, with burning eyes, and able to pick up huge buildings.

You don't argue with a Christ like that, even in a dream clearly fuelled by binge-watching Superman movies while scoffing pepperoni pizza, and so in two or three years the hospital was built. But it closed down within a decade, as Tulsa already had plenty of hospitals, as medical experts had said all along. The best you can say about this expensive episode is that the supersized Saviour might have been prompted by Roberts reading the J. B. Phillips book, *Your God is Too Small*, just before he turned in for the night.

The thing is, Oral Roberts' dream is not all that unusual. Plenty of people have had dreams of giant Jesi (the universally recognized – by me – pluralization of Jesus) and have then gone on to build them. One of those people is Father Sylwester Zawadzki, who dreamt of putting up a statue of Jesus in the small Polish town where he is the priest. He started out by wanting a statue no bigger than 'a small garden sculpture' (which in my book is basically a garden gnome), but then things got a bit out of hand and Father Sylwester ended up with a 440-ton concrete Jesus standing 33 metres tall. In fact, the Christ of Świebodzin, which was topped out in 2010 with a crown that looked like it had come out of a cracker, is the biggest Jesus in the world.

However, as it says in the book of Job, 'The Lord gave and the Lord hath taken away.' Even as Father Sylwester's Christ was having a launch-day bottle of Communion wine smashed against it, another ginormous Jesus, outside a Pentecostal megachurch in Monroe, Ohio, was going up in flames after being struck by lightning – which was most embarrassing, theologically.

The Ohio statue depicted Jesus from the waist up raising his arms high in the air, like a charismatic worshipper stuck on spin cycle. His official title was 'King of Kings', but travellers on Highway 75, which passes close by, had long nicknamed him 'Touchdown Jesus', because he looked like an American football referee signalling a goal. What no one had twigged was that Touchdown Jesus, all 19 metres of him, was made mostly of flammable styrofoam, so he was a cremation just waiting to happen.

There are 29 king-sized Christ statues in the world, each of them over 20 metres tall, the height of the *Angel of the North*. Surprisingly, eight of them are in Mexico. Less surprisingly, none of them is in Britain. Why do the statue builders want to magnify the Lord in this particular way? This was the question asked when a big bronze statue of Christ was erected on Cherubim Mountain, Syria, in 2013, in the teeth of the Syrian civil war. A local Christian leader explained, 'Jesus would have done it.' Another gigantic monument, this time a 43-metre bulletproof concrete cross, currently going up in Karachi, Pakistan, is there for essentially the same reason. The businessman behind it says it will encourage the minority Christian population: 'God will protect you. Stay in your country. Don't be afraid.'

I personally think that having to select the bulletproof option on the concrete menu could be a clue that discretion might be the better form of witness – but I'm not the man on the spot. A colossal Christ certainly gets you and your faith noticed, and not only by friendly eyes. The Cherubim Mountain Jesus, standing at an elevation of 2,000 metres, can be seen as far away as Lebanon, Israel, Palestine, Jordan – and Islamic State.

The only thing going for giant Jesi is their hulking height. Shrink any of them down and put them on a shelf in a junk shop, and they would look perfectly at home as the hackneyed art they are. But is size enough? Jesus himself was never a fan of people who look down on others from a great height. The only time he was at a great height himself was in the company of the Devil. 'Those who exalt themselves will be humbled, and those who humble themselves will be exalted,' he said. I'd rather hear those words in a pizza-fuelled dream than anything said by a 900-foot Christ.

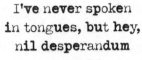

I've never spoken in tongues, but hey, nil desperandum

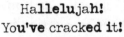

Hallelujah! You've cracked it!

21
Typing in tongues

Sitting in the passenger seat of a car the other day, going up the M6, I had a spare moment or two and decided to get ordained on my iPhone. Thanks to the Universal Life Church (motto: 'We are all children of the same universe') you can become an ordained minister in about 30 seconds flat. As soon as I completed the online form, I was whisked to a page where I could buy a personalized ordination certificate for just $8.99 to frame and put up in the toilet. Now I can open garden fetes, develop a sing-song preaching voice and obsess about the organ fund, just like the vicars on *EastEnders*. The online service has proved so popular that the Universal Life Church is producing an estimated 60 revs per hour, boom boom.

The invention and growth of the Internet has been a bit of an Alton Towers ride for Christianity since the heady days of the 1990s. Twenty years ago, most Christians, if they had heard of the Internet at all, knew it to be the infernal tool of the Antichrist, which would subjugate the whole of the world to the implacable will of Satan. Ten years later, the Internet was item 9(b) on the agenda of the church meeting: 'Progress on the church website: any news?' And today, a million dreadful websites later, churches are now tweeting the sermon, selling off the hymn books on eBay, jealously counting their likes on Facebook, and posting pics on Instagram of how an incontinent sheep wrecked the nativity play.

Along the way, there have been some inspiring moments which only religion could have brought to the Internet, such as webcam baptisms, for people who want to get baptized, don't have a nearby Baptist minister to carry it out, but do have an Internet connection and a bathful of water ready to go. Or after-rapture pet care, whereby you can make sure your beloved dog, cat or budgie is adopted after you zoom through the clouds to meet the Lord. The service is offered by atheists, who are guaranteed to still be available for pet care duties after the Second Coming.

One recent development has continued this fine tradition of theology meets technology, and it concerns the revelation of a new spiritual gift. It all came about with the sudden death of Pastor Zachery Tims, pastor of the 7,000-member New Destiny megachurch in Florida. Pastor Tims was in a New York hotel room when he abruptly died in a non-traditional fashion for a pastor by overdosing on cocaine and heroin. This left the pulpit of the New Destiny megachurch unexpectedly vacant – which is where Dr Juanita Bynum steps in. Dr Bynum is a televangelist, author, gospel singer and prophet. Some say she spent as much time and academic effort gaining her doctorate as I did on my online ordination, but that's neither here nor there.

Hearing of Pastor Tims' death, she took to Facebook and started posting prayers. She prayed not about foolish Pastor Tims, nor about the congregation he duped and scandalized, but about the plum vacancy at New Destiny megachurch, which commands a salary easily able to support a lifestyle of Manhattan hotels and crack cocaine. Dr Bynum prayed: 'YOU ARE THE ROCK AND THE SHIELD AND THE ANCHOR. WARD OFF ALL THE VULCHERS WHO WILL COME FOR GREEDY GAIN AND NOT BE CONCERNED ABOUT THE PEOPLE WHO ARE HURTING IN THAT CHURCH.' I ought to mention here that Dr Bynum always prays in ALL CAPS.

But then, thrillingly, she broke into an outburst of typing in tongues: 'WE CALL ON YOU JESUS. YOU ARE OUR HELP AND OUR HOPE!!! NDHDIUBGUGTRUCGNRTUGTIGRTIGRGBNRDRG NGGJNRIC YOU ARE OUR HELP AND OUR HOPE. RFSCNGUGHURGVHKTGHDKUNHSTNSVHGN OUR HOPE IS IN YOU FATHER.' Within hours, 2,000 people had liked her prayers.

I have to confess that speaking in tongues has never really been my kind of thing. Even as a young Christian, I couldn't help but notice that a lot of the tongues I heard sounded like a roll-call of Japanese car manufacturers: 'Kawasaki mitsubishi suzuki mazda yamaha, amen'. I even tried to get things going by repeating, 'She come on a Honda' over and over again until the Holy Ghost kicked in, but somehow, the engine would never start. Which is my loss, I'm sure.

It looks like Dr Bynum went a bit too far in trying to bring the gift of tongues to the keyboard-based world of the Internet. Some concerned Christians thought maybe she fell asleep and slumped on the keyboard, or that a cat sat on it to attend to some personal hygiene. One unbeliever commented: 'She actually typed it with her tongue.' Clearly, the Holy Ghost is not as easy as ABC. Or even QWERTY. That's a shame, because as a newly minted Internet rev, typing in tongues could have become a key part of my ministry. Which would have been very JYFUTDTRXJHLJBKHVKHV, I'm sure.

22
Nothing at all

'Which would you prefer?' asked the salesperson in the funeral home. 'Polished mahogany, with solid brass fittings and a deep velvet lining? Or maybe you'd like to consider something from our new cardboard range?' It used to be that the best jokes in the gallows humour category came from the slogans of American funeral homes, whose marketing is more robust than that of their British colleagues. They included such monuments to black comedy as, 'Don't be seen dead anywhere else',

'Let us be the last to let you down' and (my favourite) 'Thinking inside the box'.

But post-mortem hilarity has descended to exciting new depths with the advent of the flat-pack coffin, made from non-toxic cartonboard and printed all over with colourful images in tribute to the life of the funeralee. Now the coffin of Uncle Fred can proceed up the aisle looking like the Tardis, or a Formula One chequered flag bearing the word 'Finish!', or a Las Vegas fruit machine, or even a big bottle of whisky. (Come to think of it, that last option might have been an unfortunately truthful choice for at least one of my own dear relatives.) The spirit of the whole enterprise is summed up in a coffin printed up to look like a greengrocer's display of veg, crowned by a label reading, 'Rest in peas!'

Jazzed-up coffins aren't for everyone, of course, since they seem guaranteed to turn tragedy into farce, but I'm wondering if they're part of the sea change over the past couple of decades in the way the British negotiate with death. Mahogany has given way to leopardskin in the coffin department. Black ties have given way to colourful or no ties. Sombre funerals have given way to services of celebration. And speaking of the departed in hushed tones, which is how things were done when I was a kid, has given way to something altogether more upbeat.

News reports now often feature people talking about their lost loved ones by saying: 'I'm sure Mum is looking down on us and smiling right now.' Or: 'I know Dave is looking down and cheering us on in what we're doing.' Or simply: 'Rosie is in heaven with the angels, looking down on us.'

One grieving person wrote in a newsletter: 'I am sure he is looking down on us and probably thinking, wow, I have never been this high before' – but this turned out to be a report about the sad death of a snowy owl called Philly.

It's a curious idea, though. It seems that people are imagining their loved ones crowded round a TV up in heaven watching us on a Channel 5 reality show while angels come and go with cups of tea. Hardly anyone seems to say, 'She's looking down on us, totally disgusted that we've blown the inheritance on a caravan . . . or appalled at having to watch what we get up to in the bedroom.' The comedian Jack Whitehall recently offered his own thoughts on it all: 'I'm sure wherever my father is, he would be looking down on us. He's not dead . . . just very condescending.'

One thing which has reliably not changed about funerals in the past 50 years is the choice of Henry Scott-Holland's 'Death is nothing at all' for the reading. It regularly enjoys one of the best spots in the top ten of funeral readings. Henry was a canon of St Paul's Cathedral until 1918, which is when 'nothing at all' happened to him at the age of 71. He preached a sermon a few years earlier on the death of King Edward VII, and that's when he delivered his famous lines:

Death is nothing at all. It does not count. I have only slipped away into the next room. Nothing has happened. Everything remains exactly as it was. I am I, and you are you, and the old life that we lived so fondly together is untouched, unchanged . . .

Poor Henry. His sermon must be one of the most frequently abused texts in history. It actually offered a choice between two opposed ways of looking at death: is it the king of terrors, or is it nothing at all? The trouble is, Henry got carried away by his own eloquence, and his description of death being just like popping into the loo to smoke his pipe and read the latest copy of *Punch* was the one that stuck. It was soon being read out in isolation at funerals. It's unfair, but I can't help thinking that it slightly serves him right that he's only known now for the most constipated expression of English denial ever.

Henry is looking down right now, furious with himself for writing, 'What is this death but a negligible accident?' And that's how it should be. It's much better that he is raging away at something, ideally at 'the dying of the light', as Dylan Thomas says in his own funeral reading favourite.

23
What's the drill for Judgment Day?

One of the questions that isn't covered in the Alpha Course is: what do you do when the Second Coming is scheduled for next Wednesday? It's a good question, and I think it ought to be included the next time Nicky Gumbel tinkers with Alpha, because it's coming up quite frequently these days. It was a question I was pondering just a few weeks ago, on 7 October, which a Christian group had trumpeted as the date for the end of the world. But I also pondered it on 21 May 2011, when Harold Camping, a 90-year-old Californian radio show host, put the world on red alert that the rapture would definitely happen that day, just around tea time.

Mr Camping was so confident in his maths, which were reliably based on the book of Revelation, that he spent over $100 million advertising the date as 'Judgment Day' on roadside billboards. Despite the big budget, Jesus failed to keep the appointment, which was rather a blow to the people who had donated their lifetime savings to the advertising campaign. He (Mr Camping, not Jesus) then announced a new date, 21 October 2011, but when that didn't work out either, the radio show host retired in some disgrace from public life and a couple of years later went to meet the Lord in the conventional way.

That might have been that, but the man who did the PR for the failed predictions, Chris McCann, decided it was worth a third shot. He took the '1,600 furlongs' mentioned in a verse in the book of Revelation, turned them into days, added them to 21 May 2011, and – bingo! – he had a new date for the Apocalypse. He told the world: 'The Bible indicates that there is a strong likelihood that October 7th 2015 will be the end of the world.' He expounded his reasoning in a dense tract of 6,003 words which makes best sense read backwards after several large gin and tonics.

On the day itself, he had support in the unlikely figure of Jim Bakker, the televangelist who spent part of the 1990s in prison for fraud. Speaking on his post-prison TV show,

Mr Bakker told viewers that the end must be nigh, because God had instructed him to wear black: 'Even my shoes are black. My underwear is black. My socks are black.' This sadly prompted his wife and co-host Lori to give in to the sin of unbelief. 'That's too much information,' she said.

John Donne has a sonnet which wonders, 'What if this present were the world's last night?' On the morning of 7 October, I had a similar thought. What's the drill for the Day of Judgment? Take the day off work? Assemble at your nearest church? Make sure you've got clean underwear on, like your mum told you? Confess those last sins? Pack a bottle of Evian? Ring the church bells? Send some goodbye texts to unbelieving friends? Take paracetamol in case the rapture gives you the bends? No book I've ever seen by an end-times enthusiast has issued practical instructions for what to do on the day.

So I thought I'd better get down to London's beautiful Brompton Cemetery, with its 40 acres of Victorian graves, because if the Second Coming was about to kick off, it would surely start there with the general resurrection of the dead. St Paul is pretty straightforward about that. 'The dead in Christ shall rise first,' he said, and after that, 'we will all meet the Lord in the air'.

However, as I strolled between the ancient graves in the rain, the resurrection seemed to be on hold. No tombstone was toppling, no granite angel was flapping its wings, no newly raised Victorians were legging it down the cemetery paths. Instead, the crows perched on the tombstones, the rain fell on the flowers and the mighty kingdom of the dead simply kept calm and carried on.

Walking out of the cemetery I was left with another nagging question not covered by Alpha: how do I try to look reasonably sane as a Christian when my faith is being turned into a circus act by fellow believers? It's like being in a crowded restaurant and a family member at your table has just contrived to upend a giant bowl of raspberry trifle all over himself. Do you laugh along with the restaurant, or loyally try to assist your be-trifled relative? Laughing along seems the best option, as a way of saying, we're not all crazy. But there's no getting away from the fact that you're inside the splash zone, with raspberry trifle hanging off your face.

Christians have always prayed, 'Come quickly, Lord Jesus.' Maybe we should add a rider: 'Quicker, please, than the next failed apocalypse.'

You forgot to book?
Immaculate!

24
The invisible man of Christmas

'It's Christmas. You're going to be in the nativity play. What character would you most like to be?' Steve Tomkins (the esteemed editor of *Reform* magazine) and I, armed with a video camera, were stopping people in their tracks at Greenbelt a few years ago and bothering them with this festive question – in the middle of the August bank holiday weekend. Amazingly, people stopped to talk to us, and their answers were enlightening.

'I'd want to be the donkey,' said one man. 'Why?' we asked. 'I'm a bit of an ass,' he replied. We thought that was bad until another would-be standup comedian told us he would like to play that well-known cast member, the flea: 'Because Mary and Joseph had to flee to Egypt.'

As you can tell, things weren't going all that brilliantly with our out-of-season survey. But then we noticed something strange happening to two of the play's central characters. Almost every girl we spoke to wanted to be Mary, while no boy wanted to be Joseph. They were happy to be a wise man, soldier, shepherd, Herod – even the arse-end of a camel. 'Give me the innkeeper,' said one chap. 'You get a bit of attitude, a bit of shouting, a bit of door-slamming.' This is ironic, as there's actually no innkeeper in the Gospel stories. But there were no takers for the dressing gown, tea towel and flip-flops of Joseph.

You can see why. Joseph is the nice guy who gets the girl, but frankly, his best moment is leading Mary on a donkey from one bit of scenery to another, only to be upstaged by that non-existent, door-slamming innkeeper. Most of the other roles have plenty of room for pantomime. I remember one church's nativity play where the shepherds got bored sitting round their camp fire made of logs, with crinkly tinfoil for the flames, and amused themselves by popping one of the toy sheep on the fire. Joseph could never do that. He's too busy moping around after Mary and brooding on the bad hand he's been dealt by the director of the play (and by God). He's the invisible man of nativity plays.

Joseph's role is to accept the joyful news that someone got his girlfriend pregnant, her best explanation being that she met an angel. The art critic Waldemar Januszczak calls Joseph 'God's cuckold', and that's how he was often portrayed in the English mystery plays. No wonder the medieval audiences greeted him with hoots of bawdy laughter.

Could things get any worse for Joseph? Yes they could. A century after Christ, crazy folk tales of Jesus' childhood were all the rage, and Joseph didn't come out of them very well. He was depicted as a hopeless carpenter, with young Jesus having to miraculously stretch planks of wood his dad had cut too short. It's like that joke where Jesus runs to the Nazareth workshop and says, 'Dad, did you just call me?' Joseph replies, 'Oh, sorry Jesus, I just hit my thumb with a hammer.'

There was more. According to the folk stories, Mary was a virgin not only when she got pregnant, but for ever and ever afterwards. But how could this be, since she was married? The answer: Joseph was 90. You'd think this wouldn't necessarily be a problem, given all the plank-lengthening miracles going on. But in the seventh century, a church council endorsed Mary and Joseph's peculiar domestic arrangement, which the council thought was a lot more 'holy' than regular marriage.

It took 1,000 years and more before repairs began on Joseph's reputation. Since the time of St Francis of Assisi, he has been the patron saint of fathers and carpenters, and in the 1950s he was given the job of fighting against Communism by becoming 'St Joseph the Worker'. He was awarded a second feast day on 1 May, the same day the Kremlin leaders gathered on top of Lenin's Tomb in Moscow each year to review the military parade of nuclear missiles in Red Square. But on the downside, Joseph also became the unofficial patron saint of selling your house. Apparently, the best way to get a serious buyer is to bury a small statue of St Joseph upside down next to your 'For Sale' sign. The practice is so popular in the States (where you can buy a St Joseph Home Seller Kit for just $9.95, statue included) that he is known as 'God's underground real estate agent'.

So this Christmas, spare a thought for Joseph. After 2,000 years of being kicked out of Mary's bed, mocked as an old man, upstaged in nativity plays and buried upside down, it's time Jesus' dad was celebrated as the young, sexy and decent man he probably was. He deserves it. The man was a saint.

25
We need to talk about Satan

Creflo Dollar, millionaire prosperity preacher, was recently in need of a new private jet. His old Gulfstream was getting to be unreliable, forcing him to take the desperate step of travelling on commercial flights. So Revd Dollar launched an appeal to buy a new Gulfstream G650, at the very reasonable price of $65 million. When he was widely ridiculed on Twitter and the appeal was taken down, he preached an emotional sermon saying the Devil had stopped his dream purchase. It says something that Satan had to step in on this one. It seems that even the Evil One has standards, and that some behaviour is too outrageous even for hell.

Satan has enjoyed some quite exciting episodes in the extended soap opera which is church history. In medieval days, he was the red-suited monster painted on the wall of your local church. During the Inquisition, he was the dastardly mastermind behind every heretic afflicting the faith. For the Puritans, he lurked in every bubbling cauldron and directed every witch's broom like a fiendish air traffic controller. But these days, Satan has frankly become a bit of a worry.

I first noticed this when we had a new arrival in our family a couple of years ago. The new arrival's mum wanted to ask a close family friend who isn't all that fond of church if she would be one of the godmothers, and asked what I thought. 'I hope she won't mind renouncing Satan,' I said. Doing precisely that is in the small print of what godparents must do when they make their vows in an Anglican baptism. They are asked: 'Do you renounce Satan and all the spiritual forces of wickedness that rebel against God?' One possible answer to that question is, 'I didn't expect the Spanish Inquisition.'

Baptisms these days are rather jolly affairs, with cakes and presents, aunts and uncles in Sunday best, and a minister heroically struggling to hold a baby the right way up while also balancing a cup of water. What could possibly go wrong? The insistence on getting godparents to renounce Satan and all his pomps in the middle of this happy and amusing scene is like the flapping arrival of a pantomime Dracula, complete with a puff of smoke. Ta-dah! Talking to not-Christian friends about God can be uphill work these days, but mention that you also believe in God's most famous ex-employee, Satan, and you might as well have grown a second head with a matching set of horns.

But Satan is also a bit of a worry among my fellow Christians. Talking with them about him, I often encounter something surprisingly like superstition. The popular Christian belief implies that Satan, like God, is omnipresent, always on hand to plant iniquitous thoughts, dangle a new temptation or wreck your chances at following the 5:2 diet. But Satan is no god, poor creature, and can't be everywhere at once, so it's hard to see how he can fit the job description believers have set for him. Satan's dilemma is just the same as that of his fellow anagram, Santa. Not only are they both stuck with wearing red suits, but just as Santa has to hand-deliver presents to all the world's children on one single night, so Satan has to visit everyone on earth, night and day, to personally tempt them. So many sinners, so little time! How does he do it?

And what goes for Satan also goes for Satan's little helpers, the demons. It's not their metaphysical existence which is most concerning, but more a question of staffing. How the heck is hell managing to field enough demons to tempt 7.3 billion people these days? The human population is now 20 or 30 times greater than it was in the days of the Bible, but the size of hell's infernal bureaucracy has stayed the same, since, according to Jesus, angels (even fallen ones) don't get married and have babies. So the logistical problems of providing a personalized service of 24/7 temptation for everyone alive must be diabolical.

Could it be that Christians are simply expecting too much of Beelzebub? Or is it that Christians have always too readily believed in Satan's own inflated PR? After all, it's much easier to say that the Devil blocked my $65 million jet purchase, than that God stopped me from being a beyond greedy charlatan. Blaming the Old Nick is a very convenient way of getting the spotlight off your own sins.

Maybe the truth of it all is that Satan is like a teenager posting on the Net from his poxy bedroom in Clapham, pretending he's a huge corporate player. Or maybe he's even less than that. Last year, Paddy Ashdown, hearing of the sad death of Charles Kennedy, commented on his alcoholism by saying, 'We all have our demons.' It was a familiar and handy metaphor about human weakness and failure. Just like Satan.

The text for my
sermon today
is . . .

DO NOT DISTURB

26
Rev revelations

The other day, I was pondering the often surreal lives of
the clergy. They are often the subject of news stories and
private comment, and sometimes for the most interesting
reasons. For sporting tattoos. For celebrating Communion
in high heels. For developing a sing-song preacher's voice.
For swinging a smoking thurible through 360 degrees.
For leading the congregation in prayer for the healing of
someone's leg, without spotting that it was a wooden leg.

What prompted this was a story I heard over breakfast, which almost caused me to pebble-dash my iPad screen with a mouthful of porridge. It was about a would-be young vicar, turned down by a prospective church even though he offered to do the job for free. The reason? The parishioners feared that his youthful preaching would quickly swell their numbers, and then they would have their precious church car park spaces nicked by newcomers. It's comforting to know that even while churches are haemorrhaging members across the country, their car parks are reassuringly full of spaces. Praise the Lord!

The most curious episode I've ever stumbled upon in the weird and wonderful lives of church leaders came about when a friend and I were doing a sketch show tour in America and stopped off at an Episcopalian church in New Jersey. I needed to 'use the restroom' (as Americans delicately put it) before the show, and asked a couple of the jolly older women in the kitchen – all of them getting sandwiches and cakes ready for the end of the evening – where it was. They pointed me in the right direction, and then one of them cryptically added, to much hooting of laughter from them both, 'Make sure the pastor hasn't been there before you.'

'Why on earth?' I asked.

'Because of the floaters,' she laughed.

It took a couple of minutes to establish that we hadn't fallen into one of those yawning gaps between English English and American English, where you can walk down the street in your pants, and where a 'fanny pack' is a bumbag. For all I knew, the woman in the church kitchen might have been talking about a strawberry ice cream float carelessly left on the restroom windowsill. But no. What I thought she couldn't possibly have meant, she actually had meant. The vicar was famous among his parishioners for the occasional log surprise, chocolate dreadnought or ocean-going Twix, which simply would not depart in peace, even when the *Nunc Dimittis* was intoned over it.

I must confess that I sometimes fell asleep during classes when I was in theology college, so I can't be 100 per cent sure that this precise subject was covered during pastoral studies. But it definitely should be. Who knows what is talked about over the church washing-up?

I mention it because Twitter recently burst into life with a stream of revelations from clergypeople around the world about their real working lives. Casting caution and dog collars to the wind, and using the hashtag #realclergybios, they spilt the beans about the frustrations and exultations of life in the clergy frock. One minister, Catherine, took the opportunity to disclose the dietary habits of the modern priest: 'What I have eaten today: Five miniature Kit Kats, some leftover Communion wafers and a packet of cashews I found in my desk.' Meanwhile, pastor Melissa tweeted the randomness of doing theology in a beauty salon: 'Yes, I will talk about gay marriage with you while you wax my eyebrows.'

It's clearly tough being a rev, especially when it involves receiving 'anonymous notes on my desk just after preaching, with biblical texts telling me why the message I just preached was wrong', as happened to Revd Lou.

Perhaps that's why pastor Hallie tweeted, 'The first drafts of all my sermons have to be redacted for swear words' – which is probably an exaggeration, but maybe not by much.

Several priests outlined how they respond when people ask, 'What do you do?' in casual conversation. 'I'm in life insurance,' said a priest on a date. 'I'm in consulting,' said another, to the person in the next seat on a plane. The penalty for being theological (rather than economical) with the truth could be severe, as one pastor, Steve, explained: 'Why yes, stranger next to me on the plane, I did want to hear your life story for the whole flight once you learned I was a minister.'

It's not exactly breaking news to learn that our clergy sometimes want to disappear when they get the chance. Who wouldn't, with the joys and griefs, expectations and absurdities floating in their direction each day? Floating, that is, just like that unexpected surprise lurking under the lid in a New Jersey church.

Have I told you the one about the constipated camel?

To be honest, Jesus, I don't think that's going to make it into the Gospels

27
Does Jesus have GSOH?

The shortest verse in the Gospels is famously 'Jesus wept', but how about 'Jesus laughed'? Did that ever happen? Can faith be funny? Does the Holy Ghost make people split their sides? Has God got a sense of irony? I've been thinking about these questions for quite a lot of my life, but they remain questions, because Christianity, from the Spanish Inquisition to Westboro Baptist Church, has been rather famous for its sense of humour failures.

One person for whom these were not theoretical questions last month was retired teacher Albert Voss, from Münster, Germany. Albert is an atheist who likes to advertise his non-faith via the medium of funny, home-made car bumper stickers. One of them read, 'Jesus, our favourite artist: hanging for 2,000 years and he still hasn't got cramp.' Probably the most offensive thing about that is that it isn't very funny, even by the legendary comedy standards of Germany.

But the stickers landed Albert in court, where he was convicted of blasphemy and obliged to cough up €500. I was surprised to learn that blasphemy is a criminal offence in Germany, just as it is for eight other EU countries. It was a good job Albert didn't drive his weak jokes about Jesus and the Pope around Ireland, where his wallet could have been relieved of up to €25,000.

We Christians seem to be in two minds about religion and humour. About the same time Albert was appeasing the Almighty with a cash payment, someone posted the following thought on Twitter: 'Did Jesus have a sense of humor? I'm sure He did. Can you picture a camel trying to go through the eye of a needle without laughing?' Well, yes, I can. No offence, Jesus, but it would be miraculous if a 2,000-year-old joke could still raise a weak smile, let alone a genuine laugh.

Most Christians I know think Jesus could be funny. It's quite widely accepted that he did the first-century equivalent of standup, with gags such as the gnat and the camel doing the backstroke in someone's glass of wine, or routines such as the man happily walking round, oblivious to the great big plank of wood hanging off his face. But when you think about it, having a good sense of humour

(GSOH) isn't just about being funny. If someone on a dating website includes 'Must have GSOH' in their list of requirements, they don't just mean, 'Must tell lots of jokes'. They also mean, 'Must be able to take a joke'. There's a big difference.

So what about Jesus? Has he got GSOH? Did he mind having his leg pulled by the disciples? Is he OK if people crack jokes about walking on water? Did he find the crucifixion scene in *Life of Brian* funny? Is he cross if Christians involuntarily laugh when someone exclaims, 'Jesus Christ on roller skates!'? Did he mind that whenever I used to see Robert Powell in *Holby City*, I thought, 'That's what Jesus would look like as an OAP'? To adapt a well-known saying of Jesus, did he laugh at others as he would have them laugh at him?

Something tells me that quite a lot of Christians would object to those questions, because they hold that even mild jokes about our Lord are blasphemy. That's really unfortunate when you think about it, because if humour only goes one way – as in Jesus poking fun at the scribes and Pharisees – then it makes him someone who laughs at others but goes ballistic when they laugh back. Then God looks like he has all the easy, self-deprecating humour of Kim Jong-un.

It's not clear, reading the Gospels, whether Jesus really did have GSOH as we know it. But what is clear is that whenever the Church has access to significant political power, it loses any sense of humour it might have possessed. That's why we still have the legacy of blasphemy laws in Europe, with churches resisting their repeal.

Maybe we need to make up our minds about God. Are we going to embrace the radical New Testament idea that Jesus was truly one of us, with all that implies for giving and taking humour? Or are we going to stick with a more Old Testament kind of God: distant, grumpy and making a note every time someone says 'OMG!'? The answer is important because it goes to the heart of the vexed issue of religious offence.

Edward Abbey, the American author and hellraiser, once said: 'Jesus don't walk on water no more; his feet leak.' On the spectrum of humour, that is possibly a shade darker than Albert's not very funny bumper sticker. But it's a joke I think Jesus can take, without reaching for a thunderbolt.

She's been impossible since she was made Archdeacon

28
A pomposity of clerics

I was standing in the crowds outside Westminster Abbey one afternoon in 2010, waiting for the Pope to arrive in his 'bulletproof ice cream van', as one Twitter user had unkindly nicknamed the Popemobile. As the holy vehicle drew up (sadly not playing the chimes of 'Greensleeves'), a host of banners on our side of the road jostled each other for Pope Benedict's attention. They made interesting reading. Half of them hailed him as 'Holy Father' or 'Your Holiness', while the other half denounced him as the Antichrist. It was a reminder that whatever fancy title you might claim for yourself, there's always someone who will call you something different.

A *pomposity of clerics*

Clergypeople have been awarding themselves grand titles and styles of address for the best part of two millennia. The Church's bowing and scraping handbook says you should address a pope as 'Your Holiness', a cardinal as 'Your Eminence', an Eastern patriarch as 'Your Beatitude' and an archbishop as 'Your Grace'. Personally, my favourite-ever clergy honorific belonged to Bishop Madison of the House of Prayer for All Nations, an American Pentecostal church. Until his death in 2008, he was saluted by his adoring congregations as 'Precious Precious Sweet Sweet Daddy Madison'.

Many clergy titles – from prebendaries and archdeacons to exarchs and archimandrites – use words no normal human being understands. They exude an aroma of grandeur and sanctity, but some frankly leave a bit to be desired. So the leader of the Scottish Episcopal Church, who is known as the Primus, has always sounded to me like a little camping stove struggling to warm a saucepan of baked beans.

Archbishop George Carey once threw a reception at Lambeth Palace for the Coptic Pope (one of whose titles is the unassuming 'the Thirteenth among the Holy Apostles'). It was attended by the top brass of several other churches. As things drew to a close, a photographer lined everyone up for a group portrait, but in a scene worthy of Monty Python, he struggled to fit all the dignitaries into the frame.

'Your Reverence, if you could stand a little closer to His Beatitude,' he requested, 'and Your Eminence, if you could move in towards His Grace?'

That left only the Superintendent of the Methodist Church to slot into place. 'I'm very sorry,' said the photographer. 'I don't know how to address you.'

'Just call me Bill,' said the Superintendent.

Historically, an effective way to insult a church leader was to go for his honorifics, so to speak. This happened in the 1549 English prayer book, in which a prayer reduced the Pope to a mere bishop and threw in an insult for good measure: 'From the tyrannye of the Bishop of Rome and all his detestable enormities, Good Lorde, deliver us.' The prayer was later dropped for going too far.

Only two or three decades ago, traditionalists were still insisting on high doses of deference in concluding a letter to top clerics. When writing to an archbishop, the correct ending was, 'Kissing the sacred ring'. For a cardinal, it was 'Kissing the sacred purple', and for the Pope: 'Kissing the sacred foot'. Thankfully, greeting the clergy today, especially Nonconformist and Low Church reverends, doesn't involve a lot of kissing. But *Debrett's* still advises that a letter to a Catholic archbishop should end, Uriah Heepishly: 'I have the honour to be, Most Reverend Sir, Your obedient servant . . .'

In church life, special forms of address have only ever been for the ordained. Curiously, no one else – church wardens, PCC members, elders, treasurers, caretakers, church magazine editors, the people who make the after-service tea or take up the collection – is awarded this honour. Maybe it's time it changed. Next time you see your church treasurer, why not address him or her as 'Your cost-effectiveness'?

The trouble with ecclesiastical deference is that it goes hand in glove with privilege and secrecy. Grand titles and exaggerated greetings have played their own insidious part in making the clergy untouchable – even by the police – until recently. The Scottish theologian William Barclay, who died in 1978, once said, 'For some extraordinary reason, the Church moves in an atmosphere of antiquity. I have no doubt that it makes for dignity; I have also no doubt that there are times when it makes for complete irrelevance.' We now know it makes for much worse than that.

A Sufi mullah, Nasreddin, who lived in the thirteenth century, was once approached for advice by a warrior who had conquered his town. 'Mullah,' said the warrior, 'I want to award myself a splendid honorary title. It needs to have the word "God" in it, just like the great conquerors of the past, such as "God's Warrior", "God's Soul" or "One With God". Do you have any suggestions?'

Nasreddin looked at him and said, 'How about "God Forbid"?'

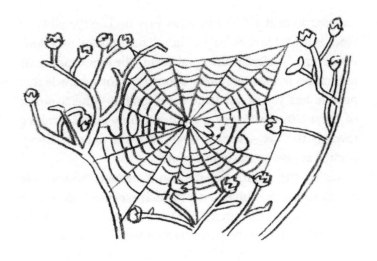

29
Christian porn

A parrot popped up in my Twitter feed a few days ago. He was raising his head from his own feed (a bowl of sunflower seeds) and fixing me beadily with a meaningful look. Right next to his grinning beak were the words of Psalm 34: 'O taste and see that the Lord is good.' This was a bit unexpected, as parrots are normally associated with, 'Who's a pretty boy then?' or 'Pieces of eight! Pieces of eight!', neither of which is found among the sacred words of the psalmist.

Because I've done a lot of time in the evangelical world, I've often encountered pious posters of sunsets, mountains, waterfalls and fjords, all of them with Bible texts improbably hanging in mid air. The heavens may declare the glory of God, as the Bible says, but for the religious poster, they don't declare in sufficiently scriptural detail. The urge to add texts to pictures is so strong that it's something of a miracle that no one has yet adapted the most famous Athena poster of the 1970s – showing a woman tennis player strolling towards the net – with a verse from the Song of Songs printed across, er, the tennis court.

But it's the pictures shared on Facebook, where cute animals endorse Bible verses, which especially deserve a place in one of the circles of Dante's Inferno. There's the fluffy white kitten, its paws clasped together, to illustrate 'Pray without ceasing'. There's the hermit crab settling into a new shell for 'The Lord is a refuge in times of trouble'. There's two pandas fighting over a bamboo shoot for 'Share with those who are hungry'. There's even a swan flapping its wings for 'Take away the foreskins of your hearts'. How anyone could make that particular connection is way above my theological pay grade.

The link between animals and piety is nothing new; the far-fetched stories of the saints of old also have their Narnia-like moments. St Ciarán built an Irish monastery with the help of a fox, a badger and a wolf. St Eustace, a second-century centurion, was converted by a stag carrying a lit-up cross between its antlers. St Francis preached to the birds, while his junior, St Anthony of Padua, preached to a shoal of fish, who all poked their heads out of a river to catch his drift. It was once believed in the British Isles that cattle knelt in their stalls on Christmas Eve, while the bees hummed a hymn to the newborn Saviour of the world.

Possibly inspired by these touching scenes, a Southampton vicar in the 1990s hit on the great idea of introducing live animals into his church's annual nativity play. Church often makes animals nervous, with results requiring a mop and bucket, but no one was prepared for what happened when Mary and Joseph arrived at the Bethlehem stable. 'The donkey developed a huge and distracting erection,' reported the vicar. So much for 'Little Donkey'.

It's a blindingly obvious thought, but no donkey in that condition would ever make it onto a poster with a Bible verse – which of course is fair enough. But interestingly, neither would a shark, wasp, piranha, tarantula, python, vulture or velociraptor. They're all God's creatures, but their horrible tea-time habits are just a bit too jarring to match the feelgood theology. That's why scorpions and cockroaches aren't exactly top of the bill in the evangelical zoo.

Instead, the animals that make the grade are the pin-ups of the animal kingdom: majestic elephants, cute koalas, comical crabs, puppies which look like they have never disgraced themselves on a shagpile rug, and the kitschiest creature of the whole Internet, the kitten. Put them together with the most sanitized Bible verses known to man (or woman), and what you get is sickly sweet Christian porn.

One final creature might provide a theological antidote, and it's the owl. I'm not talking about the baby owl, which is basically a tiny, adorable feather duster with huge eyes, but the fearsome predator it becomes, swooping silently in the dead of night. The Welsh poet and priest R. S. Thomas conjures up this phantom in his poem 'Raptor', where he sees in the owl a neglected image of God.

> I have heard
> him scream, too, fastening
> his talons in his great
> adversary, or in some lesser
> denizen, maybe, like you or me.

Those unsentimental lines are a lot closer to the God of Scripture and experience than 'Be still and know that I am God', endorsed by a sloth. 'He's wild, you know,' says Mr Beaver in *The Lion, the Witch and the Wardrobe*. 'Not like a tame lion.' Mr Beaver is right. Except that even a lion is a bit too cute to show us God.

More **WD40,**
vicar?

30
Bots on pews

One of the great theological questions I never got answered when I was in Sunday School was, 'How does Jesus get my collection money?' The question arose whenever I put a couple of warm pennies in the collection plate and we sang the Victorian children's hymn:

> Hear the pennies dropping,
> Listen while they fall,
> Ev'ry one for Jesus,
> He shall have them all.

What bothered me was that Mrs Fidelia H. DeWitt, who wrote the hymn, specifically promised that Jesus would get every single penny. Even Geraldine, the Sunday School teacher I secretly fancied, wasn't able to offer a cast-iron explanation of how this could happen, so I came up with my own theory. There must be some sort of supernatural slot machine where you put in your pennies for Jesus and they come out in heaven. I even imagined Jesus beaming with holy satisfaction as my pennies dropped into his lap. Messiah and mechanics working together made perfect sense to me.

It looks like machines which work even greater wonders than the supernatural slot machine might soon be an intrinsic part of our lives, including our churches. Driverless cars, android butlers offering Twiglets to party guests, drones walking your dog, and android shop bots greeting you by name as you wander into Boots – all of them are just a few months or years away, depending on which soothsayer you believe. Just last month, Shimon, a four-armed robot which plays the marimba and jams improvisational jazz, was the toast of YouTube.

Some technologists think this could be more than a bit worrisome. Elon Musk, the man behind SpaceX, the company developing rockets to colonize Mars, says the arrival of artificial intelligence (AI) is potentially more dangerous than nukes. He fears that our brilliant machines will one day see humans as nothing more than irritating spam, and delete us all in a desktop-tidying apocalypse.

The Church has a limited history of contact with robots, but one of its most intriguing encounters was at the medieval abbey of Boxley in Kent, where there was a mechanical Jesus. The wooden figure, nailed to a cross, was controlled by monks pulling hidden wires and levers to open and close his eyes and mouth. Was he just a creative bit of theatre to illustrate what happened on Good Friday? Or did the monks operate him to frighten gullible pilgrims into giving their own pennies to Jesus? No one quite knows. What is sure is that the Rood of Boxley, as the figure was known, became famous and gained the abbey a lucrative reputation as a place of miracles.

When Thomas Cromwell's agents arrived in 1538 to strip the abbey of its treasures for King Henry VIII, they found robot Jesus and realized he was propaganda gold for their quest to discredit the old faith. They put him on display, denounced him as a money-making idol, smashed him to bits and threw him on a bonfire. And they elaborated the story of what he could do, such as moving his hands and feet, nodding his head, pulling a grimace and rolling his eyes. All of which shows that fear of robots is nothing new.

A few church leaders have been wondering aloud whether androids who turn up for church on a Sunday should be welcomed in the traditional way with a hymn book and a limp handshake. Revd Christopher Benek, a church pastor in Florida, believes Jesus died for our tin-pot friends just as much as he did for you and me. He also thinks they would make excellent preachers. He asks: 'Who is to say that one day AIs might not even lead humans to new levels of holiness?'

Meanwhile, theologian James McGrath wonders: 'Could an android be baptized (assuming that rust is not an issue)? Could one receive Communion? Could one be ordained? Could one lift its hands in worship? Could an android speak in tongues?' But he also worries that if a robot got converted to fundamentalism, it might go Dalek and order everyone to follow literally all the laws in the book of Leviticus. For those who refused to obey, it would be, 'Excommunicate! Excommunicate!' I think it's more likely that church bots will go wrong in smaller, more irritating ways. It's not hard to imagine an e-curate standing at the front, blowing a fuse and saying, 'And also with you', over and over again.

While androids will probably be coming to church in the near future, it might be a bit soon to start debating whether they should be ordained. Maybe they could start with something more modest, such as joining the coffee rota or taking up the collection. If one could also be programmed to deliver every penny personally to Jesus, that would make me very happy.

31
Swell to great

Do you ever wonder what it must have been like back in baroque times to be at the church where J. S. Bach was the organist? Me neither. But come to think of it, I can just imagine the first time old J. S. performed his newly composed Toccata in F Major. It's a flabbergasting tsunami of sound more suited to the great and dreadful Day of Judgment than a quiet Sunday morning in church. Afterwards, standing at the door as the congregation reeled out in shock, the minister might well have put on a

Michael Caine voice to tell Bach: 'You were only supposed to blow the bloody doors off.'

It's no surprise that a church member of the time said that if Bach carried on like that, either the organ would fall to bits or the congregation go deaf. I know something of what they meant, as I grew up on an enriched diet of J. S. Bach myself. Our church's organist was my dad, and he held a passion for the great composer, just like the character Organ Morgan in the Dylan Thomas play *Under Milk Wood*. When Organ Morgan's wife asks him over supper which of two of their neighbours he likes best, he rouses himself from a musical reverie to say: 'Oh, Bach without any doubt. Bach every time for me.'

When he was just 14, my dad took over organ duties at his Welsh village church, because the regular organist went off to fight Hitler. Growing up, I was bewitched by the way his hands leapfrogged between the three manuals of our church organ – choir, swell and great – and how his feet tap-danced on the pedals. When I sat at the controls myself, I discovered what it was like to tangle with a contraption that requires all four of your limbs to move in different directions at once. The experience is like being half an octopus. And I was intoxicated by the power of being in sole charge of a 16-foot pipe which rumbles like an earthquake and throbs so deeply it could take down the walls of Jericho by verse 2 of 'Guide me, O Thou great Jehovah'.

The leaders of the Protestant Reformation weren't very nice about the church organ. It would be a refreshing change to report that they mildly observed that organs 'aren't such a great idea' or 'maybe we should try guitars instead'. But no. As in everything, John Calvin and others thundered that they were the Devil's bagpipes and should be smashed to bits with axes and sledgehammers – which people who were understandably sick of bagpipes were only too happy to do.

Just to make matters worse, some Catholic theologians agreed, saying that organs were novel, noisy, theatrical and even lascivious. Yet despite all the hostility, the organ prevailed, mainly because Protestant worship had vast amounts of psalm and hymn singing, and the instrument proved brilliant at getting people to sing the notes in the right order.

What the Protestant Reformers overlooked was how hair-raisingly holy the organ can be in the right hands. Played with quiet intimacy, it echoes the still, small voice heard by Elijah. Played with bright confidence, it's the very soul of Luther's 'A mighty fortress is our God'. And with all the stops out, it whips up a musical thunderstorm as potent as the fiery, cloudy pillar leading the Hebrews out of Egypt, or Moses descending Mt Sinai, his face glowing like the luminous green dial of an alarm clock.

But sometimes, of course, the merry and mighty organ falls into the wrong hands, and that's where holiness gives way to hilarity. This happened in a Glasgow kirk one Sunday, where the organ had never before been fired in anger. That morning, as the elders solemnly processed up the aisle, the organist, who had recently quarrelled with them, struck up 'Send in the clowns'. A similar case of organ spamming afflicted a funeral mass at St Frances de

Chantal in Brooklyn, New York. The deceased had been a heavy drinker, and the organist discreetly saluted him with 'Roll out the barrel'. One of the mourners commented, 'Nobody in the congregation noticed the tune, except the priest, who had to hide his face behind a service book for laughing.'

In churches, abbeys and cathedrals, the theme tunes of *The Magic Roundabout*, *The Simpsons* and *Blackadder*, as well as the songs of Kylie Minogue and others, have issued from the pipes of church organs, slowed down and tarted up by their intrepid players to sound like sacred songs and solos. You can't help feeling that Bach would admire their virtuosity. But at the same time, Calvin must be feeling highly smug that he was right all along about the Devil's bagpipes.

I think they use
the Emoji Bible

32
A Bible in emoji

It's smiley faces all round, as news has broken that the Holy Scriptures have at last been translated into emoji. For Martian readers, emoji are the colourful little symbols humans use on their smartphones, including winking faces, red hearts, kissing lips and praying hands. Zach Swetz, who works in social media, developed the Bible (presumably during a slow patch at work) by taking the text of the King James Bible and replacing words such as 'king', 'spirit' and 'wine' with a crown, a ghost and a glass of red plonk. So far, so forgettable.

What makes the story interesting is that after the Emoji Bible was released, Zach asked the media not to name him, because he was being trolled by excitable believers who said his work was helping to 'usher in the Antichrist'. You can see why the believers were getting a bit above themselves with their anathemas, because Zach has basically reduced the Scriptures to a series of banal, clip-art moments. David slays Goliath? 🙂 Jesus dies on the cross? 🙁 Moses parts the Red Sea? 😄 Mary puts baby Jesus in a manger? 🖤 This is a Bible with all the subtlety of a pair of over-inflated Botox lips.

Zach shouldn't have been surprised by the negative reactions to his new Bible, as it has ever been thus. In Reformation times, the traditional way to welcome the publication of a new Bible translation was to throw as many copies as possible onto a crackling bonfire and dance round the flames in righteous glee. That's what happened to the Bibles of Wycliffe, Luther and Tyndale, and so the Emoji Bible, in its tiny way, is in better company than it deserves to be.

Even the mighty King James Bible, on first publication in 1611, had its fair share of hate mail. A good quantity of that came from the Puritan scholar Hugh Broughton, who said he 'had rather be rent in pieces by wild horses' than see the new Bible put into English churches. For the avoidance of doubt, he added: 'I require it to be burnt.' A whole edition of the King James Bible (1,000 copies in all) was eventually thrown on the fire in 1631, when one of the Ten Commandments was printed as, 'Thou shalt commit adultery'.

The King James was actually a flop when it first hit the streets. That's because people were happy with their old Bibles. The new version put a line through the more colourful verses in William Tyndale's translation of 90 years earlier. A particular loss was the way the snake speaks in the Garden of Eden. When Eve tells him she and Adam will die if they eat the forbidden fruit, Tyndale's serpent responds, 'Tush, ye shall not dye.'

There was a time when the only Bible in town was the King James Bible, and the attitude was, 'If it was good enough for St Paul, it's good enough for me.' But then in the 1970s and 80s, a whole slew of new Bibles started to hit the shops, and whenever one did, you could rely on Revd Ian Paisley to strip off his shirt and start shouting about it. The Living Bible was the Living Libel, he said, while the New English Bible was a per-version. Thankfully, 'big Ian' has now gone to rest from his labours, and the timing of that has been pretty great, as the Lord alone knows how many cappuccinos' worth of froth he would have spluttered over the Emoji Bible.

You can't really compare the King James with the Emoji, of course. If the King James is Guinness, brewed by experts, then the Emoji is a craft beer, cobbled together by enthusiasts. But like the unpredictable products of micro breweries, craft Bibles are eccentric and fascinating. For instance, bits of the Bible have been translated into fictional languages such as Klingon, of *Star Trek* fame, as well as Quenya (or Elvish), presumably so the elves of Tolkien's Middle Earth can get on with evangelizing Mordor.

Then there's the Bible in L33t (pronounced Leet), an alternative alphabet for ageing computer geeks who used to get a kick out of substituting numbers and other keyboard symbols for letters, just like everyone now does for pa55w0rds. So John 3.16 looks like this: 'F0r G0d $0 l0v3d th3 w0rld, th@t h3 g@v3 hi$ 0nly b3g0tt3n $0n, th@t wh0$03v3r b3li3v3th in hi|v| $h0uld n0t p3ri$h, but h@v3 3v3rl@$ting lif3.'

Producing new Bibles used to land people in jail, or on top of bonfires, because the book was so important. But now it just lands them *Daily Mail* headlines and oodles of free publicity, and only if they're comic novelties, rather than Bibles to be reckoned with. And that, according to the most up-to-date version we now have, is very 🙁 .

Go forth and
multiply . . .

Maths

33
The dating of the
New Testament

The dating of the New Testament is one of the most vexed areas of biblical scholarship. Some scholars argue for early dates and others for late dates, but as far as I can see, the problem of New Testament dating is that there's just not very much of it. Despite there being a good number of promising 20-somethings in the Jesus pack – e.g. Mary and Martha, James and John – any sexual chemistry that might have been bubbling away is written out of the gospel story. Maybe the sons of thunder weren't that cracking after all?

Even the stories of Jesus which sound a bit like the title of a dodgy DVD, such as the Parable of the Ten Virgins, turn out to be perfectly innocent. One old preacher, expositing this very parable (in which a group of bridesmaids at a wedding are scheduled to greet the bridegroom with lighted lamps), sternly asked his congregation: 'Where would you rather be: in the light with the five wise virgins, or in the dark with the five foolish virgins?'

The lack of New Testament dating might have come about because Jesus said his ideal follower would be a 'eunuch for the kingdom of heaven' – which as far as I know is not a relationship status setting on Facebook. Or maybe it's because St Paul told people not to even think about getting married, unless their pants were literally about to explode in a ball of flame. When it comes to sexual attraction, the New Testament just rolls over and goes to sleep.

But how different everything is over in the Old Testament! It's like having a raucous lap dancing club next door to a Strict Baptist church. There's Samson and Delilah, Ahab and Jezebel, David and Jonathan, and of course Adam and Eve. There's Potiphar's wife trying to seduce young Joseph. There's marriage fiend Solomon, with his 700 wives, plus 300 concubines in a state of DEFCON-5 readiness. There are the Old Testament's industrial levels of begetting. There's gorgeous young Abishag, who was appointed to be

King David's hot-water bottle when he was old and couldn't get warm in bed. All in all, the first half of the Bible is like Las Vegas: 'What happens in the Old Testament stays in the Old Testament.'

It also has the *Kama Sutra* of the Scriptures, the Song of Songs, which doesn't have a lot to do with singing, but does have maybe a bit too much organ practice. The Song, an oriental love poem, has stoutly resisted attempts by the theological police to eject it from the Scriptures. But like the nude statues in the Vatican, it has only kept its place with the help of a fig leaf, which is that the Song of Songs is really the love story of Jesus and the Church.

In one of the many unbuttoned moments of the book, the beloved's breasts are admiringly compared to a pair of young deer romping in the lilies. How on earth could this refer to the Church? Let John Gill, eighteenth-century Calvinist, explain: 'By these breasts may be meant the two Testaments, the Old and the New, which are both full of the milk of excellent doctrines.' And therein lies the problem. If the Song of Songs is all about Jesus fancying the Church, what do you do with the bedroom scenes? They simply have Too Much Information for the pious angle to work without collapsing into comedy. For example:

Jesus and the Church are lying on their bed of cedar.
A turtle dove coos in the rafters.

Jesus: Your stature is like that of the palm, and your breasts like clusters of fruit. I will climb the palm tree. I will take hold of—

The Church: Not tonight, Jesus. I've got a headache.

Given the way the New Testament likes to keep its sheep and goats segregated, while the Old Testament loves to bung them together, it's no wonder Christians have been conflicted on the subject of sex. On the one hand are websites which offer clueless Christian males biblical chat-up lines, such as: 'So last night I was reading in the book of Numbers, and then I realized, I don't have yours.' On the other hand is the advice offered to teenagers dancing too close during the slow songs: 'Leave room between you for Jesus.' And on a (hypothetical) third hand is a lonely hearts ad posted in an Exeter newspaper, which can only be applauded in its search for a Pentecostal soulmate: 'Born again Christian lady, 43, seeks loving gentleman with the gift of tongues.'

If it's all a bit of a mess, then it's a mess of biblical proportions.

Take, eat . . .

34
The Everlasting Arms

A priest walks into a bar and asks the barman to give him a Hail Mary. 'Don't you mean a Bloody Mary?' replies the barman. 'And two Our Fathers for insulting the Blessed Virgin,' says the priest.

The relationship between priests and barmen, and between churches and pubs, has got quite complicated in the past few decades. As congregations shrink and people increasingly need binoculars to see if anyone else is in the faraway pews of their monster Victorian churches, the buildings have been boarded up, then pulled down or flogged off, and some of them have been turned into pubs. The C of E has got rid of some 1,570 surplus houses of the Lord since the end of the 1960s.

Anxious ecclesiastical bureaucrats have tried to fathom what's gone wrong by putting the Church under the microscope – they've had to, it's that tiny now. And the trend has prompted theologians to ask, 'How many denominations can dance on the head of a pin?' and the answer is, 'All of them, even the ones that forbid dancing.'

And so it has come to pass that Muswell Hill Presbyterian Church is now an Irish pub called O'Neill's, where dirgy organ music has been ditched for live rock'n'roll, and bread and wine for Peroni and pork scratchings. But the traffic isn't entirely one way. A bullish Diocese of London struck back in the 1990s by planting a new church, Church on the Corner, in a derelict Islington pub, the King Edward VII, and it hasn't turned back into a pub yet.

This game of musical chairs by pubs and churches was anticipated way back in the eighteenth century by William Blake, who penned a subversive poem, 'The Little Vagabond', which says:

> But if at the Church they would give us some ale,
> And a pleasant fire our souls to regale,
> We'd sing and we'd pray all the livelong day,
> Nor ever once wish from the Church to stray.

To which I'd only add, throw in live rugby on a jumbo plasma screen, and it's a deal. I've always harboured a secret ambition myself for turning a pub into a church and calling it 'The Everlasting Arms'. Even though it's highly unlikely that will ever happen, I've started to collect the names of beers which would lie most happily in the cellar of my dream pub church. To start with, there's a beer brewed in Salt Lake City, the capital of Mormonism, which rejoices in the name of Polygamy Porter. Its marketing slogan? 'Why Have Just One?'

Following that, there's a whole heavenly host of baptized beers. You can sup a pint of Saint Cuthbert in Durham, order a Grim Reaper and a bag of crisps in Gloucester, chug a Churchyard Bob in Warwick or a Revd James in Cardiff, and even put away a glass of All Creatures Bright and Beautiful, as brewed by the aptly named Black Sheep Brewery. Then there's Bishop's Finger, Monty Python's Holy Grail, William Wilberforce Freedom Ale ('produced for the 200th anniversary of the Abolition of the Slave Trade') and Sin Boldly, with a picture of Martin Luther on the bottle. Luther enjoyed his Wittenberg ale so much that he gave it this joking justification: 'Whoever drinks beer is quick to sleep. Whoever sleeps long does not sin. Whoever does not sin enters heaven. Therefore let us drink beer!'

There are two patron saints of beer in the British Isles: St Arthur Guinness and St Jack (C. S.) Lewis. Arthur was a Dublin saint who lived at a time when getting trashed on cheap gin was the toxic temptation of the working poor. The enticement was: 'Drunk for a penny. Dead drunk for twopence.' As a good Methodist, Arthur spotted a highly profitable opportunity to save people from the gin bottle, and started brewing a stout which evolved into the black, creamy elixir which eventually put his name in gold on a billion beer glasses.

Meanwhile, St Jack Lewis did his bit for beer and belief by getting in some serious time at the Eagle and Child in Oxford, downing bitter and enjoying holy smokes with fellow saints J. R. R. Tolkien and Charles Williams. The booze and fags side of the creator of Narnia is a bit uncelebrated, to my way of thinking. Three pints and a bit of chain smoking over lunch is hardly standard material for the life of a saint, but then standard saints aren't capable of writing books such as *The Screwtape Letters* and *The Lion, the Witch and the Wardrobe*.

Maybe it's time to rewrite that joke. C. S. Lewis walks into a pub and asks the barman for a White Witch Surprise. 'Why on earth do you want one of those?' asks the barman. Lewis replies, 'Narnia business.'

HYMNS
2 5 1
6 2 8
X X X
9 3

35
Bosoms and ebenezers

In the words of the continuity announcements on Channel 4, this column may contain strong language and scenes of a sexual nature from the start. Our subject this month is sex and hymns. You might not think sex has much to do with hymns, but just like Samson and Delilah, the two of them enjoy a surprising amount of intercourse.

And therein lies the first problem with many hymns written in Victorian and earlier times: old-fashioned English is the double-entendre's friend. Most churches know this and have wisely stopped talking about

Sexagesima Sunday (the Sabbath-but-one before Lent), if only because it used to triple the number of excitable people cramming into church. Thrillingly, the Sunday after Sexagesima is Quinquagesima, which just has to be an item in the connoisseur edition of *The Joy of Sex*.

I've always found singing in church a joy, but some hymns make you smile for all the wrong reasons. For a start, they use words that lead very different lives in other parts of your brain. Words such as 'bare', 'bondage', 'bosom', 'bowels', 'breast', 'bush', 'desires', 'conquest', 'flesh', 'gay', 'kiss', 'loins', 'lover', 'organ', 'prostrate', 'queen', 'rude', 'seed', 'submission', 'succour', 'tossed', 'virgin', 'womb' – and not forgetting good old 'intercourse'. Or as the hymn writer William Bathurst put it: 'Let our hearts, from sin made free, Hold sweet intercourse with thee.' Try reading those lines out with a steady voice as you announce the hymn. I'm sure my first-ever encounter with most words from the lexicon of love happened while I was singing in Sunday School, which must make the hymn book a crash course in sex education.

One candidate for Hymns Ancient and Freudian is the old standard, 'Fill Thou my life, O Lord my God', with the awkward lines, 'Praise in the common things of life, Its goings out and in', which have been known to make people spray Baptist Communion cordial over the pew in front. It doesn't exactly help that the man who wrote these words rejoiced in the name of Horatius Bonar. Another fine example is the 'Alleluia' verse for the Twentieth Sunday after Trinity. A former chorister who sang the words, said: 'It took me a bit by surprise, as I was expected to respond to the versicle with, "I will sing and give praise with the best member that I have."'

These days, vicars and ministers wisely omit the offending verses from suggestive hymns, but sometimes the wrong verse is taken out. This happened to me recently when we were singing 'All things bright and beautiful'. We sensibly omitted the verse about how we gather rushes by the water every day, but unaccountably left in the verse concerning 'the purple-headed mountain'. On the same subject, I remember leaving church one Sunday after we'd sung 'Come, thou fount of every blessing', with its stirring line, 'Here I raise my ebenezer'. At the church door, a perplexed friend asked the minister, 'How exactly does one raise one's ebenezer?' He was advised to see his doctor.

Some hymns are so littered with innuendo, they must surely test the humour reflexes of even the stiffest and starchiest saint. Take the lovely, lively hymn, 'Thou didst leave Thy throne and Thy kingly crown': all goes well until you hit the line, 'But Thy couch was the sod, O Thou Son of God'. Another lengthy hymn, 'Jerusalem, my happy home', springs the following surprise in verse 23:

> Our Lady sings Magnificat
> With tune surpassing sweet,
> And all the virgins bear their parts,
> Sitting at her feet.

And then there's the serene and sleepy children's hymn, 'Now the day is over', which waits until verse 4 before delivering this heartfelt prayer:

Grant to little children
Visions bright of Thee;
Guard the sailors tossing
On the deep blue sea.

Even the most treasured songs aren't immune from sacred smut. Try keying into Google the bold declaration, 'We like sheep'. You'd think the search results would show the top ten jokes about the dating habits of Welsh shepherds, but instead we get the famous duet chorus from Handel's *Messiah*, which has been known to reduce school-age choristers to tears of laughter.

Hymn book publishers over the past 50 years have been quietly dropping anthems which are just too eccentric now. Their cull has deprived us of hymns such as 'The happy eunuch', 'The Earth is gay', 'What was it made my bosom swell?' and a splendid eighteenth-century specimen, 'Blest is the man whose bowels move'. Even the Victorians realized this line was open to a second meaning, so they edited it to 'Blest is the man whose breast can move', which was so much better. Personally, I think the hymn censors should leave well alone. Our hymns are fabulous just as they are, bosoms, ebenezers and all.

36
Twerking comes to Narnia

The first time I ever clocked a Wayside Pulpit was on my way to school one morning. There on the wall of the local Methodist church as I sauntered past in short trousers was a poster in Dayglo orange and black lettering which asked, 'CH--CH: What's missing?' Below this question were the letters 'UR'. I fell in love with the farcical side of Christianity on the spot.

Since then I've seen many cheesy church signs, but one of my favourites ever was put up by the Socastee Baptist Church in South Carolina: 'God is the Potter, not Harry.' I especially love the idea that the surname of a fictional character could be seen as an affront to a metaphor about God, but that's the gloriously demented logic of church billboards.

It's no accident that this sign was in the Deep South, as the Bible Belt didn't exactly warm to the novels of J. K. Rowling. A fundamentalist list of Satan's favourite things currently circulating on the web includes ouija boards, vampirism, marijuana, Halloween, fornication and Harry Potter. In fact, 'the Harry Potter series convinces me that the Antichrist is not far off'. That's the sober opinion of John Hagee, Texan megachurch pastor and end-times aficionado.

This state of affairs created a dilemma for at least one Southern mom, who wanted to protect her children from all the godless evolution, feminism, atheism and Devil-worship there is in children's books these days. Posting on the Net as proudhousewife, she wrote: 'My little ones have been asking to read the Harry Potter books . . . but I don't want them turning into witches! So I thought, why not make some slight changes so these books are family friendly?'

And that's how *The Hogwarts School of Prayer and Miracles* came into being. Proudhousewife's novel begins like this: Harry is living with his aunt and uncle when Hagrid knocks on the door to ask if the family have been saved. Aunt Petunia, a career woman wearing a 'baggy, unflattering pantsuit', says they don't need God as they already have Dawkins, but Harry is eager to know more. 'Then pray the sinner's prayer!' booms Hagrid. Harry is saved in ten seconds flat and becomes a Bible-quoting, virginity-toting automaton. Proudhousewife is especially against women who fail to dress, cook and clean for their husbands. She finally abandoned the novel when her own husband declared that her writing wasn't good for their family.

Fan fiction, where readers take their favourite novels and add brand new chapters full of fundamentalism, comedy, sex scenes, prequels, missing episodes and alternative endings, is a thriving and fascinating area online. Harry Potter leads the field for fan fiction, but Narnia, with its big cast of characters, human and beastly, isn't very far behind. There are almost 12,000 additions and corrections to C. S. Lewis's creation on just one of the fan fiction websites, enough to keep him spinning at high speed in his grave for several thousand years. They range from full-blown novels to scraps you could write in big letters on a postage stamp, and their content ranges just as widely.

Thus Lucy snogs Tumnus the faun; Susan learns to cope with iPhones and twerking; Puddleglum gets married; Caspian plays cricket on board the *Dawn Treader* until Lucy knocks a six into the sea; Edmund calls on J. R. R. Tolkien in his Oxford rooms; Susan has a lion carved on the gravestones of her three siblings after their train disaster; everyone (including Peter) falls in love with Caspian; Aslan sends Reepicheep out of Narnia and onto the Starship *Enterprise* of *Star Trek* 'for a joke', and Susan knocks on the door of the Tardis, only to be ignored by Doctor Who.

Stories about Susan, the sister of Peter, Edmund and Lucy, feature a lot in Narnia fan fiction. That's because there's a widespread feeling that C. S. Lewis treated her shabbily, and the fans push back in her defence. Susan is the only sibling who fails to make it to Aslan's Country in the final Narnia book, and it's partly because 'she's interested in nothing now-a-days except nylons and lipstick and invitations'. Yes, Susan discovered sex and so there's no heaven for her. It's a bit vexing to see the way Christianity pairs so easily with casual misogyny, either by being introduced to Harry Potter by proudhousewife, or written into Narnia by one of the Christian heroes of the twentieth century.

My favourite Narnia rewrite is *The Lion, The Witch and the Chevrolet Equinox*, in which the former presenters of *Top Gear* get into a chevvy for a between-filming cigarette break and find themselves sitting down in Narnia. Jeremy Clarkson exclaims: 'And the back seat appears to have a forest in it. That's going to completely bugger up the suspension.' It's not very C. S. Lewis, but just occasionally, that's a bit of a relief.

CAR PARKING
Anglicans: free
Baptists: free (inc. car wash)
Atheists: £10 per hour

37
Will Jesus find me a parking space?

I found a 'Jesus space' the other day while I was circling the soulless car park of my local B&Q. This is something to celebrate, because a Jesus space is a parking spot blessed over all others. It's the space which is closer to the door of the shop than any other space, excluding disabled parking.

The life of a Christian believer is one of constant sacrifice and self-denial, but on the plus side, a well-known perk is that Jesus will find you a parking space. Either Jesus, or if he's not available, his mum. There's even a handy steering-wheel prayer to cover it: 'Holy Mary full of grace, help me find a parking space.' One conservative Christian blog shares the joy of steering into a divinely vacated space: 'The moment you pray to find a parking space, a car drives away from the store's front door. We shake our heads in wonder and say, Wow! That was a miracle.' Wow indeed.

The love affair between Jesus, Mary and motors is so strong in modern Christianity that it's practically a shock to find it's not covered in the epistles of St Paul. Almost since its invention, the automobile has been a sort of travelling shrine, as celebrated in the 1950s American folk song, 'Plastic Jesus', in which the singer doesn't care if it rains or freezes as long as he has his plastic Jesus on the dashboard. (Making 'Jesus' rhyme with 'freezes' reminds me of the 'Praise Cheeses' headline in a tabloid newspaper, after the face of our Lord was discovered in a pizza. Thanks brie to God for that.)

Meanwhile, for the evangelical believer, who shrinks from the sight of a religious statue, even a plastic one, with as much horror as Superman does from green kryptonite, there's always the fish bumper sticker, which turns your car into a four-wheel advert for Christianity. Sadly, cars with fish stickers are usually driven insanely or parked with their bottoms angled out into the road. Maybe it's because they've just been sold to heathen drivers who have fought a losing battle with prising the sticker off the paintwork. But the stickers are such a fixture of Christianity, I wouldn't be surprised if swanky chariots on the roads of the Roman Empire 1,500 years ago also carried fish signs, causing as much mystification to the driver behind then, as now.

An exciting new growth area in the world of motoring seems to be healing for cars. After all, if faith can move mountains, what about fixing my carburettor? One man whose car had a leaking petrol tank heard a sermon about faith in Winners Chapel, a prosperity gospel megachurch in Nigeria. He said, 'I stepped outside the service and quietly went to my car and began to speak to the fuel tank. After lunch I checked and behold, heavenly mechanics had soldered the leakage without my having to pay a dime. Hallelujah to Jesus for this awesome testimony.' I think it's traditional to let others decide whether your testimony is awesome, but even so, I must remember to give my petrol tank a pep talk next time I fill up.

Another believer, this time from Florida, said God blessed him with a 'supernatural gas increase'. This sounds alarming to an English ear, especially if the miracle is bestowed in a confined space, but mercifully the testimony clarifies things. 'I took my family on a trip to Orlando for a vacation and back. I also went to work and church. I did six hours of driving for only $40 of gas. That's a miracle! It multiplied! Jesus is Lord!'

No account of motors and miracles, of bangers and believers, would be complete without 'Jesus, take the wheel'. This country song about a woman whose car (and life) is spinning out of control until she hands the steering wheel to the Lord has since gone on to become a rather less than reverent exclamation for whenever things go slightly wrong. One woman who maybe took 'Jesus, take the wheel' a bit too literally as she drove her Ford sedan in Okaloosa County, Florida, closed her eyes to pray and then kept them closed as she ran a stop sign, mounted the pavement, crossed a lawn and embedded the car in the side of a house. Amazingly, no one was hurt in this story where 'watch and pray' seems to have gone out the window.

These days, whenever I see a free parking space outside B&Q or elsewhere, I take it God is being ironic. It's our little joke. 'Want me to find you a parking space, or make the double yellow lines disappear?' he nudges, po-faced. 'You think you're so funny,' I reply. Jesus once said, 'Why worry? All the hairs of your head are numbered. God knows every sparrow which falls.' And every parking space you'll never find.

Left a bit,
left a bit . . .

38
The Christingle banana

A few days before Christmas, a woman posted on Mumsnet in a state of utter bafflement. The question she posed was eye-catching: 'A satsuma, a candle, two raisins, a sweet, four cocktail sticks and a peanut . . . what?' Her daughter had just come home from church school 'with the above items in a bag, and is on about putting the candle in the satsuma, and gluing on the sweet and raisins. She then is supposed to light the candle every day. Any idea what she is on about or what it all means?' Another mum sympathized: 'What on earth have jelly babies stuck in oranges got to do with Jesus?'

Christians these days have a lot on their hands with unbelievers asking difficult questions such as, 'If God is a God of love, why is *Songs of Praise* still on the telly?' So it's something of a trial at Christmas when you also have to explain the connection between Jesus and jelly babies. (It must also be a trial for all the people named Christopher Tingle on LinkedIn, of whom there are quite a few, but let's not intrude on their grief.) How did it come to this?

The Christingle, cause of mystification on Mumsnet and focus of children's services on various Sundays in December, is a curious beast. Its cocktail sticks, tin foil, candle and bits of ribbon (not to mention jelly babies), all lashed together on an orange, look like an out-of-control Sputnik that's got tangled up in a load of space junk and then caught fire.

Its eccentric appearance is matched by its fruit and nut symbolism. It can't seem to make up its mind which season of the church year it's talking about, a bit like a cantankerous uncle who won't pick a lane on the motorway, despite the kindly blasts on the horn of other drivers. The red ribbon is for the blood Jesus shed on the cross, so that's . . . um . . . Easter. The bits of food impaled on the cocktail sticks are for the fruits of the earth, which is, well, Harvest. And the four cocktail sticks themselves symbolize the four seasons, which is Vivaldi. So remind me, someone: how in the name of Bassetts Jelly Babies is this meant to be a Christmas thing?

The Christingle banana

The Christingle is a surprisingly recent arrival in church history. Its ingredients didn't emerge miraculously from the mists of time-honoured tradition, but were brought together in 1968 by Mr John Pensom, a Children's Society fundraiser, who was rather a character. When he died in 2006, the *Church Times* obituary revealed that on his letterhead he had once styled himself as John Pensom DGO. He admitted to friends that the DGO was in fact that well-known honour, the Damned Good Organizer. As things turned out, Mr Pensom needn't have bothered about gongs and awards. That's because his fruit-based marvel was enthusiastically embraced by British churches, and he became affectionately known as Mr Christingle, which is a lot better than having a DGO.

Admittedly, John Pensom wasn't creating *ex nihilo*. He adapted his idea from a Moravian bishop, Johannes de Watteville, who gave children lighted wax candles wrapped in a red ribbon for a service in Christmas 1747. How and when de Watteville's simple idea transmogrified into the bloated Holy Orange of the present day is not hard to fathom. It's the tin foil and cocktail sticks which give it away. In the late 1960s and early 70s, every middle-class party featured a cheese and pineapple hedgehog, which was half a grapefruit covered in tin foil and bristling with cocktail sticks, with big chunks of cheddar and tinned pineapple skewered on the spikes. You don't have to be Clouseau to spot that the Christingle is basically the love child of Christmas and terrible 70s party snacks. It's a miracle that Twiglets weren't added to symbolize the wood of Noah's Ark.

The fiftieth anniversary of the Christingle is coming up in 2018, and it's not too early for churches to carry out an upgrade to the Flaming Sputnik. Yes, it's time to change the fruit and let another item from the supermarket trolley point the way to Bethlehem.

My nomination is for the Christingle banana, a snack with some solid doctrine behind it. Banana skins are famously hazardous when dropped, and that reminds us of Adam and Eve slipping up over a fruit. Bananas are yellow, the colour of gold, the first of Baby Jesus' presents. The banana looks like a boomerang, which reminds us Jesus will return a bit unexpectedly. And bananas are smile-shaped, just like people smiling at Christmas parties as they're offered mulled wine, even though they're screaming inside.

The Christingle banana. It could just be the most random and ridiculous church idea ever, except for the Christingle orange.

Transubstantiate!
Transubstantiate!

39
Baptizing a Martian

There was wonderful news earlier this year when three exoplanets were discovered circling a nearby star in the constellation of Aquarius. One of the planets orbiting TRAPPIST-1, an ultracool dwarf star, might be suitable for life, and as it's only 39 light years away could be reached by Ryanair inside 53 million years, which coincidentally is how long I had to wait for my baggage to hit the carousel last time I flew with them. When astronomers were asked why they called the star TRAPPIST-1, they said their lips were sealed, boom boom.

As if this discovery wasn't enough, a few months later it was revealed by radio telescopes that another star, this time 95 light years distant, might have beamed a cautious 'hello' in our direction. Could it be that an advanced civilization is flirting with us from the constellation of Hercules? Or is that last sentence just a piece of random text from Mystic Meg's astrology column in *The Sun*?

All the talk of exoplanets and alien civilizations has put the UFO world into a spin. Almost as much of a spin as when Pope Francis delivered a homily a couple of years ago saying he would be happy to baptize Martians if they'd only meet him halfway by showing up at the Vatican. 'If an expedition of Martians came tomorrow,' he said, 'and some of them came to us here – Martians, right? Green, with that long nose and big ears, just like children paint them – and one said, "I want to be baptized!" What would happen?' Then he added: 'When the Lord shows us the way . . . who are we to close doors?'

It sounded like the Pope was getting the Vatican red carpet out of storage (and warming up the baptismal water) to welcome our green cousins. In reality, the Pope's homily wasn't really about Martians. He was talking about the Church being open to the Spirit and adapting to unexpected change, and the Martians were just there for a comedy walk-on part. But UFO enthusiasts around the globe picked up the reference, which is why the Pope's visitors from Mars quickly took on a life of their own on some of the Net's wilder websites.

Conspiracy theorists have long had a thing about the Vatican, in the same way my friend's dog Sammy once developed a loving relationship with a local vicar's leg. It's not hard to see the attraction (to the Vatican, rather than the vicar's leg). After all, the Vatican has a secret archive dating back to the eighth century, with 85 kilometres of shelving, a policy where even the index is secret, plus a labyrinth of pedantic Italian bureaucracy to defend it. The small cabal of people in charge say it contains nothing more exciting than the Pope's homework and shopping lists, but all that secrecy must hide something.

So the Vatican, the dear old thing, has effectively pinned a 'Kick me!' label on the seat of its pants, and the conspiracy theorists have responded enthusiastically. They've already decided what the archive must contain: the lost epistles of St Paul to Nero saying Jesus was a fiction; a time machine used by a monk to go back to the crucifixion and film it; and of course, negotiations between the Holy Father and our future alien overlords on microchipping the human race. The beauty of a secret archive is you can make up whatever you think must be in it.

There have also been some much-quoted comments about aliens from officials in the Vatican Observatory. Father Guy Consolmagno, who among other things is Keeper of the Pope's Meteorites (not a euphemism), is maybe too positive about dishing out Communion wafers to Klingons. 'Any entity, no matter how many tentacles it has, has a soul,' he opines, adding that he would baptize any galactic visitor as long as it said please. He's even written a book, *Would You Baptize an Extraterrestrial?*, and gave it that title because it's one of the top questions people ask him. Mine would be: how would you handle a full immersion baptism in zero gravity? Or maybe I'd ask something more devotional: when God closes a door, does he open an airlock?

Will aliens turn up in our lifetime? According to a survey published by the Royal Society, if ET was found, Christians don't think their personal faith would be blasted to atoms, but they do think the Church might struggle to defend its traditional beliefs. So top marks to the Catholic Church for giving the Martians some thought. On the other hand, even the arrival of aliens on a rocket-propelled Ford Mondeo seems more likely than the unlocking of the Vatican's Secret Archive. Which is lovely for the conspiracy theorists, but for hardly anyone else.

40
In praise of holy fools

Western Christianity boasts some eccentric forms of religion, perhaps most famously the Pentecostal snake-handling churches of the Appalachian Mountains. Their favourite Bible verse isn't John 3.16, but the one where Jesus says in passing that his future followers would 'take up serpents' without harm. Unfortunately, the rattlesnakes they take to church don't hold the same interpretation of this proof text, with the result that quite a few believers have perished.

Snake-handlers aside, most of Western Christianity is an utter bore compared with the wild eccentricities of the

Eastern Church. Orthodox monks and nuns have lived up trees, in barrels, in bricked-up chapels or out in the fields grazing like sheep. St Simeon the Stylite started a craze among Syrian monks by balancing on top of a 50-foot pillar, drawing huge crowds and practising a kind of divine vertigo. He was so revered that even his blessed number twos, as they plopped off the pillar, were piously collected and turned into medallions for the faithful. Which only goes to show that you *can* polish a turd.

You'd think such extreme saints had reached the far end of austerity. But there was one final feat of mortification, and even the toughest men and women of the desert were in awe of it. It was the calling to be a fool for Christ. The first of these mavericks was another Syrian saint, Simeon the Holy Fool, who lived quietly as a monk in a Dead Sea cave for 29 years. But then one day he set out for the city of Emesa. He had decided to mock the idiocy of the world and convert sinners by becoming a public fool.

During church services, he pelted the clergy with nuts. In the circus, he wrapped his arms around the dancing girls and went skipping across the arena. In the streets, he tripped people up and dragged himself around on his buttocks. In the bath-house, he ran naked into the crowded women's section. On solemn fasting days he feasted riotously on beans, with predictable results. The locals saw him as a madman and beat him when his antics proved too much.

The tradition of fools for Christ really took off when it arrived in Russia. The Russian fools endured not only destitution and beatings, but also went naked in the cruel

Russian winters. For them, being seen with a hot-water bottle would have been as scandalous as the Archbishop of Canterbury being found in the bosom of a stripper.

Russia's most famous holy fool, St Basil, found his vocation in shoplifting, giving stolen goods to the poor and rebuking Tsar Ivan the Terrible for being a bit too terrible. In a sense, his mission of foolishness failed, because he ended up being buried honourably under the crazily colourful onion domes of St Basil's Cathedral in Red Square. In contrast, Rasputin, who is sometimes claimed as a holy fool (although he was actually an unholy scandal), ended up full of bullet holes and floating face down in a river, which would be a holy fool's dream ending. Rasputin had a reputation for healing and generosity to the poor, but also for heavy drinking and visiting brothels, and I only mention him because his story highlights the dangerous game genuine holy fools played with hypocrisy, masochism and actual madness.

Fools for Christ are rare in our time. At the height of the Cold War, St Gabriel the Holy Fool, a priest-monk from Tbilisi, Georgia, burned a giant portrait of Lenin during a Communist May Day parade. He was beaten by the crowd, tortured, sentenced to death and finally declared to be a psychopath. His response was to become a full-blown holy fool, masquerading as a drunkard and preaching loudly in the streets. Icons of St Gabriel, who died in 1995, show him smiling sweetly, which is a rare sight in the severe world of Orthodox icons.

If you were a bog-standard monk or nun, you waved a fond farewell to home, family, shopping, cakes and sex.

If you were an uber-saint like the stylites, you also said goodbye to the ground. But holy fools went even deeper into the spectrum, and found the ultra-violet of holiness as divine lunatics, outsiders and troublemakers. They added one more impossible thing to their vows of poverty, chastity and obedience, and that was humility to the point of humiliation.

A woman once found St Gabriel weeping in a church. He told her why: 'Christ was born in a manger, but people respect me and kiss me on the hand.' The favourite Bible verse of the holy fool is the one where St Paul says, 'We are fools for Christ.' Maybe the snake-handling Pentecostals could adopt it. But not just them, of course. Me too.

Tyler's Story

A little story about learning to read in prison

It's probably my drinking that got me into prison. That and not having a proper job.

I wasn't bothered about school, but in prison I had a chance to join a reading group. The books are interesting but not too hard to read.

In one book, *Forty-six Quid and a Bag of Dirty Washing*, we read about Barry, a guy who got mixed up with a drug dealer, but has now just left prison. I saw how he had to make good choices every day – and fill in lots of forms – to stay out of prison. I don't want to end up back inside again, so I've decided that I'm not going to drink on my way home. I won't get home drunk before the evening's even started – that just makes me drink more. And I'm going to get better at reading so I can fill in forms when I get out.

Inspired by a true story. Names have been changed.

Help us to tell more stories like Tyler's. Support the Diffusion Fiction Project. Just £4.99 puts an easy-to-read book in prisoners' hands, to help them to improve their reading confidence while encouraging them to think about life's big questions. Visit www.spck.org.uk to make a donation or, to volunteer to run a reading group in a prison, please contact prisonfiction@spck.org.uk.